WEEKEND MAKES

CROCHETED TOYS

25 QUICK AND EASY PROJECTS TO MAKE

WEEKEND MAKES

CROCHETED TOYS

25 QUICK AND EASY PROJECTS TO MAKE

EMMA OSMOND

First published 2019 by
Guild of Master Craftsman Publications Ltd
Castle Place, 166 High Street, Lewes,
East Sussex, BN7 1XU

Text © Emma Osmond, 2019
Copyright in the Work © GMC Publications Ltd, 2019

ISBN: 978 1 78494 549 7

A catalogue record for this book is available from the British Library.

Senior Project Editor: Kandy Regis
Managing Art Editor: Darren Brant
Art Editor: Lindsay Birch
Photographer: Jesse Wild
Stylist: Jenny Howard

Colour origination by GMC Reprographics
Printed and bound in China

CONTENTS

Introduction   6

Crochet Basics   7

Crochet Terminology   16

Information   17

PROJECTS

Loop Rattle   18

Comfort Blanket   20

Cloud Cot Toy   28

Star Mobile   33

Teddy Bear   36

Bunny Rabbit   42

Octopus   48

Giraffe   52

Elephant   58

Unicorn   64

Sensory Toy   70

Bean Bags   74

Stacking Rings   78

Stacking Cubes   84

Colour Game   88

Number Disks   94

Finger Puppets   102

Super Soft Ball   112

Skittles   117

Car   122

Aeroplane   130

Tic-Tac-Toe   134

Fishing Game   138

Toy Basket   143

House Doorstop   146

Index   150

Acknowledgements   152

INTRODUCTION

What better way to use some beautiful soft yarn in an array of colours than to make some of the fabulous crocheted toys featured in this collection of 25 patterns? There's something for all the little ones here – from a comfort blanket, baby rattle and cot toy for the very tiny, to games and toys for toddlers.

There are animals galore in the collection – an enchanting elephant, a beguiling bunny and an awesome octopus, not forgetting a rather gorgeous giraffe and a very unique unicorn.

And when it's time to play, there are all sorts of games you could conjure up with your crochet hook. Of course there are some that are purely just for fun, like the finger puppets, skittles and fishing game, but there are others that will help the youngsters to learn as they play, such as the colour game and number disks.

So, whatever the age of the child and whatever your skill level, whether you're new to crocheting or an old hand, you will find a project to hook up with here that will become a treasured toy in a little one's life.

Emma Osmond

Crochet Basics

Here you will discover all the basic stitches you will need to crochet the projects in this book, including double crochet, half treble crochet, treble crochet and slip stitch. We will also look at crochet skills such as increasing and decreasing, joining two pieces together, making a ring and working stitches into a ring.

DOUBLE CROCHET

Double crochet is one of the most common crochet stitches. A fabric made of all double crochet stitches is fairly dense and solid, ideal for snuggly yet durable essentials such as comfort blankets, animal toys and cot mobile decorations that will brighten up the nursery.

1 Insert the hook into the stitch that you want to work.

2 Take the hook under the yarn.

3 Pull the hook back through the first loop on the hook (two loops on hook).

4 Take the hook under the yarn again.

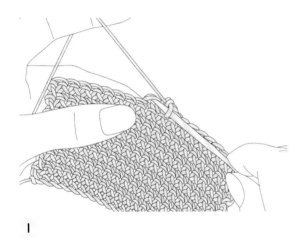

1

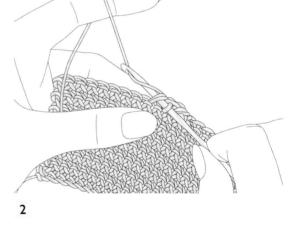

2

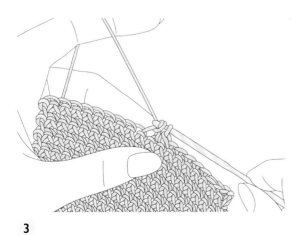

3

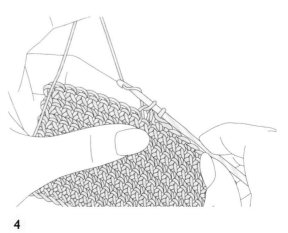

4

5 Pull the hook back through both of the remaining loops on the hook.

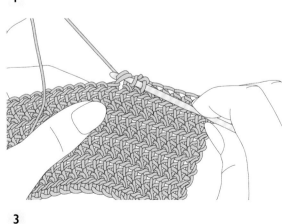

6 Here is a finished sample worked in double crochet.

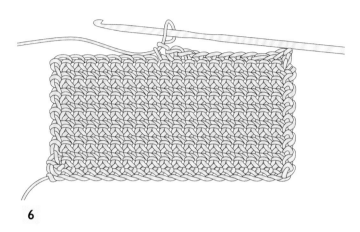

HALF TREBLE CROCHET

The half treble crochet is half way between double crochet and treble crochet. It produces a firm, durable fabric that is used in many patterns.

1 Wrap the hook under the yarn.

2 Insert the hook into the stitch that you want to work.

3 Take the hook under the yarn and back through the first loop on the hook (three loops on hook).

4 Take the hook under the yarn and bring it through all three stitches at once.

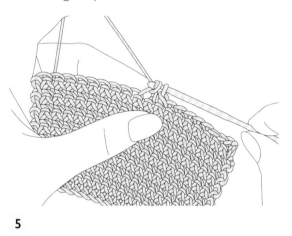

1

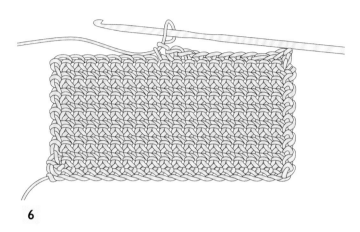

2

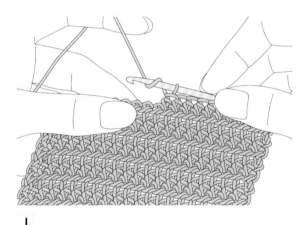

3

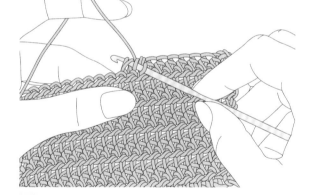

4

5 This is how the finished half treble stitch should look.

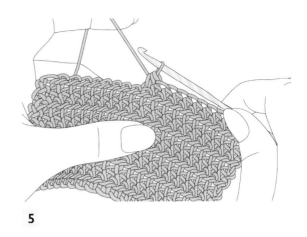

5

TREBLE CROCHET

Treble crochet produces tall stitches, which can create a more open fabric in no time at all.

1 Place the hook under the yarn and insert the hook into the stitch that you want to work.

2 Wrap the hook under the yarn again and come through the stitch (three loops on hook).

3 Wrap the hook under the yarn again and pull through the first two loops, wrap the yarn under the hook and pull through the remaining two loops.

4 This is how the finished treble stitch should look.

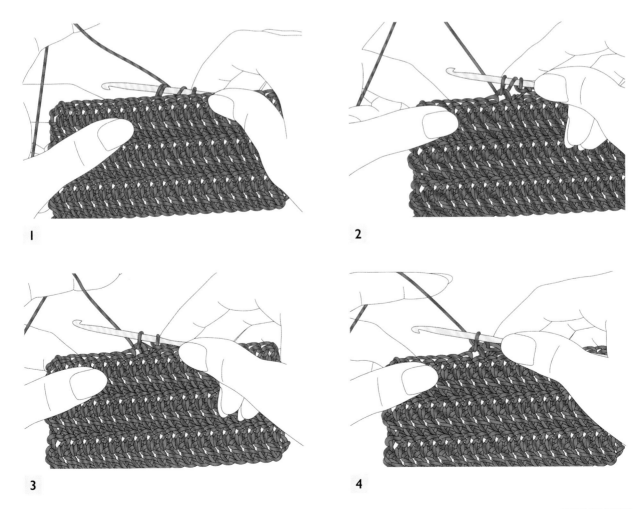

1

2

3

4

SLIP STITCH

The slip stitch is used to move along your work and to join rounds. It is useful when working motifs.

1 Insert the hook into the next stitch.

2 Wrap the yarn under the hook.

3 Bring through both stitches on the hook. You have now completed a slip stitch.

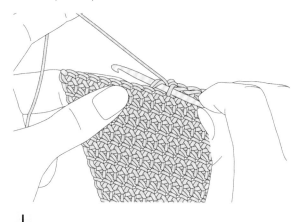

1

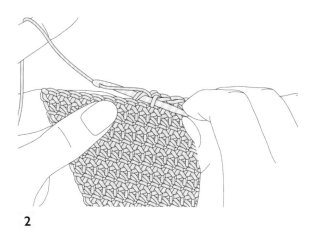

2

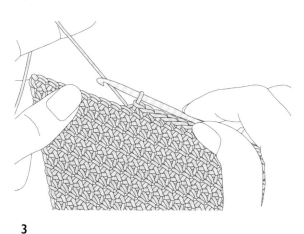

3

JOINING IN A NEW YARN COLOUR

There are many different ways of adding a new colour to your work, depending on the type of stitch you are using. The slip stitch can be used for any stitch, but is best worked at the beginning of the row and not when working in the round. Here, I am working in double crochet.

1 Work until you are on the last stitch of the row. Work your stitch in the normal way until you get to the last step of your stitch (two loops on the hook). Take the new coloured yarn, make it into a loop and slip it onto the hook.

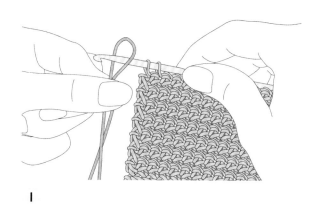

1

2 Bring the new yarn through the two loops to complete a double crochet.

3 Turn and continue to work your stitches. Cut the first yarn and knot together the two ends. You will need to sew in these ends once your project is completed.

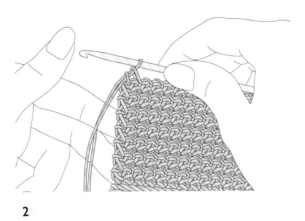

2

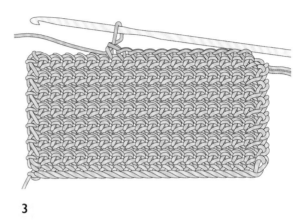

3

INCREASING

You may need to add stitches when making a toy or following a pattern. These can be added in the middle or at the end of the row – both are done in the same way. Here, I am working in double crochet.

1 Work one complete stitch.

2 Insert the hook into the same space or stitch below and work another stitch.

3 This is how the finished increase stitch should look.

4 If you increase on every row your work should look similar to this.

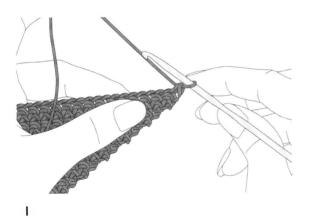

1

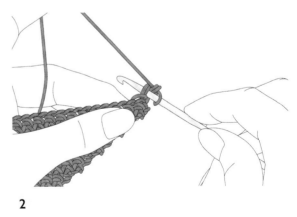

2

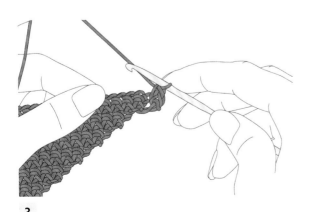

3

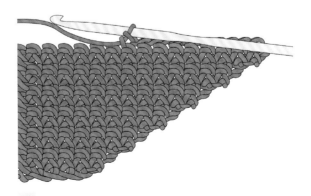

4

DECREASING

As with increasing, when making a toy or following a pattern you may need to remove stitches, which can also be worked at any point during a row.

1 Work your stitch to the last step (two loops on the hook).

2 Work a double crochet into the next stitch, up to the last step again (three loops on hook).

3 Complete the decrease by bringing the yarn through all the loops on the hook.

4 If you decrease on every row your work should look similar to this.

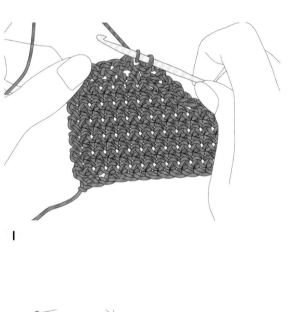

1

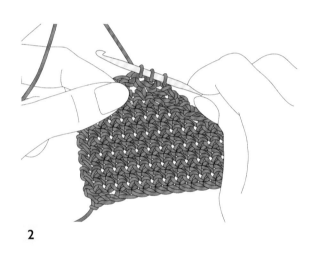

2

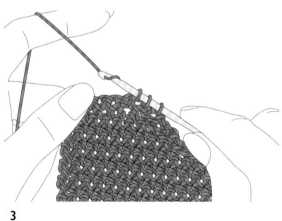

3

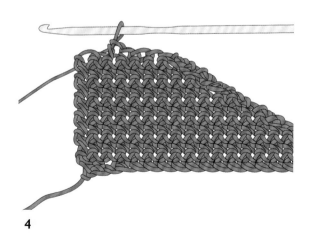

4

JOINING TWO PIECES TOGETHER – MATTRESS STITCH

There is a variety of sewn stitches that you can use to join your crochet pieces. First, sew all yarn ends in neatly and block pieces if necessary before assembling them. Use a large darning needle to stitch with.

1 Lay the two pieces next to each other, right sides up. Insert the needle from back to front in the first stitch on the right-hand side. Repeat on the left-hand side.

2 Insert the needle back into the right-hand side piece of work and up one stitch.

3 Repeat on the left-hand side and continue up like a ladder.

4 Pull tight every few rows to create a neat invisible seam.

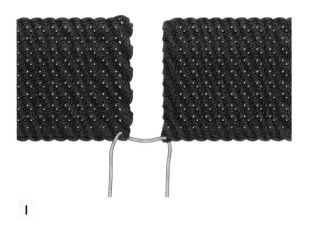

1

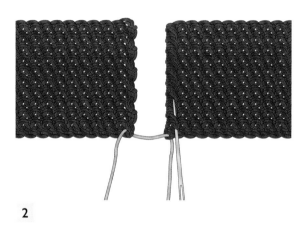

2

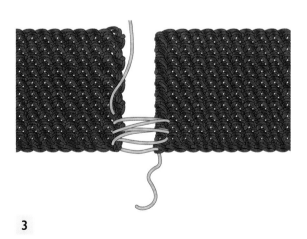

3

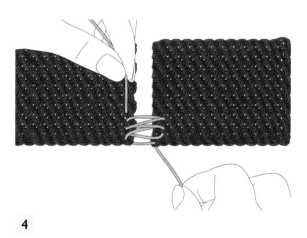

4

JOINING TWO PIECES TOGETHER – CROCHET

This variation of the double crochet stitch can also be used to join completed crochet pieces together to produce a firm, well-defined edge.

1 Hold the two pieces you wish to join with right sides together.

2 Insert the hook through both pieces of the work into the two corresponding stitches of the front and back pieces.

3 Catch the yarn with the hook and bring it through the two pieces.

4 Insert the hook into the next stitch and catch the yarn to bring it through the two pieces (two loops on the hook).

5 Bring the first stitch through the second stitch (one loop remains). Repeat Steps 2–5 until you reach the end of your work.

6 To secure your work, simply pull the tail end of the yarn through the loop on the hook.

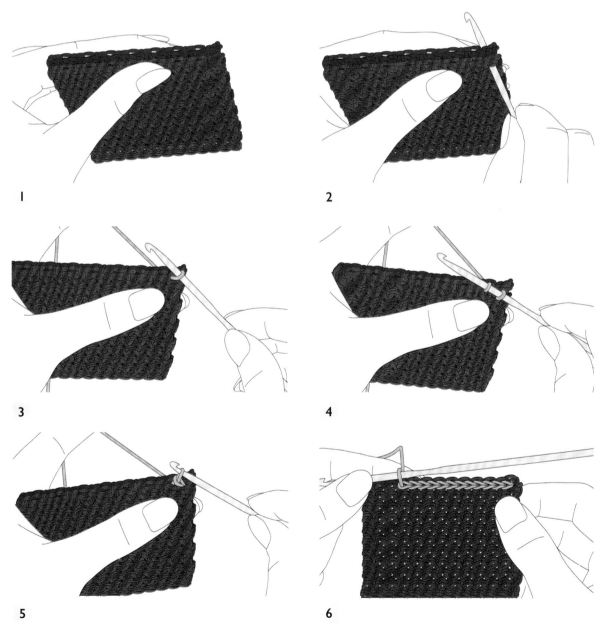

1

2

3

4

5

6

MAKING A MAGIC RING

Many crochet motifs are created by working in the round; starting at the centre and working outwards.

1 To make a ring, start by making a chain (five chains are shown here).

2 Join the ring using a slip stitch into the first chain from the slip knot. This is how your finished magic ring should look.

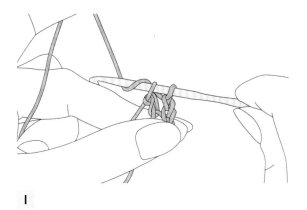

1

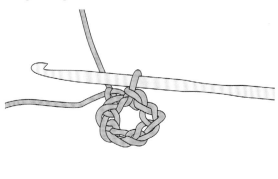

2

WORKING STITCHES INTO A MAGIC RING

Moving on from the magic ring, you will need to start working stitches into the centre.

1 Work the required number of chains to create the height of the stitch you wish to work. Here we will be using treble crochet, so three chains are required.

2 To work the stitches, simply place the hook into the centre of the ring and work a treble crochet. Continue working treble crochet into the centre ring, as required.

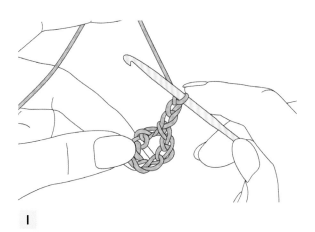

1

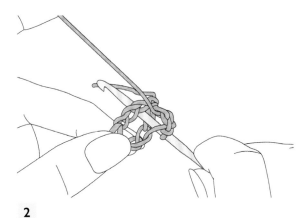

2

CROCHET TERMINOLOGY

Crochet terms in the UK are different from the US; the most common confusion arises when the same term is used to refer to completely different things. The tables below shows conversions for hook sizes and terminology.

CROCHET HOOK SIZES AND CONVERSIONS

US SIZES	METRIC SIZES (mm)
-	2.0
B/1	2.25
-	2.5
C/2	2.75
-	3.0
D/3	3.25
E/4	3.5
F/5	3.75
G/6	4.0
7	4.5
H/8	5.0
I/9	5.5
J/10	6.0
K/10½	6.5
-	7.0
L/11	8.0
M/13	9.0
N/15	10.0

UK/US TERMINOLOGY CONVERSIONS

UK	US
Slip stitch	Slip stitch
Double crochet	Single crochet
Half treble crochet	Half double crochet
Treble crochet	Double crochet
Double treble crochet	Treble crochet

INFORMATION

TENSION

Obtaining the correct tension is perhaps the single most important factor that can make the difference between a successful project and a disastrous one. Tension controls both the shape and size of an article, so any variation, however slight, can distort the finished project.

I recommend that you crochet a square in double crochet (depending on the pattern instructions) of perhaps five to ten more stitches and five to ten more rows than those given in the tension note. Mark out the central 10cm/4in square with pins. If you have too many stitches to 10cm/4in, try again using a thicker hook. If you have too few stitches to 10cm/4in, try again using a finer hook.

FINISHING INSTRUCTIONS

After working for hours crocheting a project, it seems a great pity that many projects are spoiled because such little care is taken in the pressing and finishing process. Follow the instructions below for a truly professional-looking item.

PRESSING

Block out each piece of crochet and follow the instructions on the ball band to press the project pieces, omitting the ribs. If the ball band indicates that the fabric is not to be pressed, then covering the blocked out fabric with a damp white cotton cloth and leaving it to stand will have the desired effect. Darn in all ends neatly along the selvage edge or a colour join, as appropriate.

STITCHING

When stitching the pieces together, remember to match areas of colour and texture very carefully where they meet. Use a seam stitch such as back stitch or mattress stitch for all main crochet seams, unless otherwise stated.

LOOP RATTLE

Using baby-safe 4ply yarn, these rattles are a super-quick project to make for your own children or to give as a gift to a new arrival. You can play around with colour options and stripes to suit the recipient.

SKILL LEVEL: EASY

YOU'LL NEED:

YARN
Rowan Summerlite 4ply or any No.1 super fine weight yarn
A – 1 x 50g of Pure White 417
B – 1 x 50g of Blushes 420
C – 1 x 50g of Duck Egg 419

I made all 3 rattles with the above yarn plus left overs.

HOOK
3mm (US C/2) hook

EXTRAS
Toy stuffing
Small rattle inserts suitable for children's toys

LOOP RATTLE

SIZE
14cm/5½in in diameter

TENSION
28 sts and 30 rows to 10cm/4in
Measured over double crochet using 3mm
(US C/2) hook.

RATTLE
Using 3mm (US C/2) hook and yarn A make
17 chains, join with a slip stitch into first
chain to make a ring.
Foundation round: Make 1 chain, work 1
double crochet into each stitch to end, join
with a slip stitch.
Last round sets pattern, keeping pattern
correct continue working stripe
sequence below.

Rounds 1 – 9: Yarn A.
Rounds 10 – 18: Yarn B.
Rounds 19 – 27: Yarn A.
Rounds 28 – 36: Yarn C.
Rounds 37 – 45: Yarn A.
Rounds 46 – 54: Yarn B.
Rounds 55 – 63: Yarn A.
Rounds 64 – 72: Yarn C.

MAKING UP
Stuffing as you go and inserting rattle
in centre, join edges together using
mattress stitch.

COMFORT BLANKET

Made from a washable merino and silk blend yarn, this soft cuddle blanket is great for snuggling up to. The contrasting band keeps it modern but it can also be worked in one colour with the bear, keeping it gender neutral.

SKILL LEVEL: EASY

YOU'LL NEED:

YARN
Rowan Baby Merino Silk DK or any No.3
light weight yarn
A – 1 x 50g of Straw 671
B – 1 x 50g of Frosty 702

HOOK
4mm (US G/6) hook

EXTRAS
Toy stuffing
Embroidery thread or small amount of yarn

COMFORT BLANKET

SIZE
34cm/13½in × 34cm/13½in

TENSION
15 sts and 10 rows to 10cm/4in
Measured over pattern using 4mm hook.

BLANKET
Using 4mm (US G/6) hook and yarn A make 4 chains, join with a slip stitch into first chain made.

Round 1: Make 3 chains (this counts as a treble crochet), work 2 treble crochets into ring, * make 2 chains, work 3 treble crochets into ring, repeat from * twice more, make 2 chains, join with a slip stitch into top of 3 chains.

Round 2: Make 5 chains (this counts as 1 treble crochet and 2 chains), * (work 3 treble crochets, 3 chains, 3 treble crochets) into corner chain space, make 2 chains, repeat from * twice more, work 3 treble crochets, 3 chains, 2 treble crochets into following chain space, join with a slip stitch into third of 5 chains. Slip stitch into next chain space.

Round 3: Make 3 chains (this counts as a treble crochet), work 2 treble crochets into same chain space, make 2 chains, * work (3 treble crochets, 3 chains, 3 treble crochets) into corner chain space, make 2 chains **, work 3 treble crochets into following chain space, make 2 chains, repeat from * twice more, then from * to ** once, join with a slip stitch into top of chain.

Round 4: Make 5 chains (this counts as 1 treble crochet and 2 chains), work 3 treble crochets into next chain space, make 2 chains, * work (3 treble crochets, 3 chains, 3 treble crochets) into corner chain space, make 2 chains **, work 3 treble crochets into next chain space, make 2 chains, work 3 treble crochets into next chain space, make 2 chains, repeat from * twice more, then from * to ** once, work 2 treble crochets into following chain space, join with a slip stitch into third of 5 chains. Slip stitch into next chain space.

Round 5: Make 3 chains (this counts as a treble crochet), work 2 treble crochets into same chain space, make 2 chains, work 3 treble crochets into next chain space, make 2 chains, * (work 3 treble crochets, 3 chains, 3 treble crochets) into corner chain space, (make 2 chains, work 3 treble crochets into next chain space **) 3 times, make 2 chains, repeat from * twice more, then from * to ** once, make 2 chains, join with a slip stitch into top of chain.

Round 6: Make 5 chains (this counts as 1 treble and 2 chains), work (3 treble crochets into next chain space, make 2 chains) twice, * (work 3 treble crochets, 3 chains, 3 treble crochets) into corner chain space, (make 2 chains, work 3 treble crochets into next chain space **) 4 times, make 2 chains, repeat from * twice more, then from * to ** once, make 2 chains, work 2 treble crochets into next chain space, join with a slip stitch into third of 5 chains. Slip stitch into next chain space.

Round 7: Make 3 chains (this counts as a treble crochet), work 2 treble crochets into same chain space, (make 2 chains, work 3 treble crochets into next chain space) twice, make 2 chains, * (work 3 treble crochets, 3 chains, 3 treble crochets) into corner chain space **, (make 2 chains, work 3 treble crochets into next chain space) 5 times, make 2 chains, repeat from * twice more, then * to ** once (make 2 chains, work 3 treble crochets into next chain space) twice, make 2 chains, join with a slip stitch.

Round 8: Make 5 chains (this counts as 1 treble crochet and 2 chains), work (3 treble crochets into next chain space, make 2 chains) 3 times, * (work 3 treble crochets, 3 chains, 3 treble crochets) into corner chain space **, (make 2 chains, work 3 treble crochets into next chain space) 6 times, make 2 chains, repeat from * twice more, then from * to ** once, (make 2 chains, work 3 treble crochets into next chain space) twice, make 2 chains, work 2 treble crochets into next chain space, join with a slip stitch into third of 5 chains. Slip stitch into next chain space.

Round 9: Make 3 chains (this counts as a treble crochet), work 2 treble crochets into same chain space, (make 2 chains, work 3 treble crochets into next chain space) 3 times, make 2 chains, * (work 3 treble crochets, 3 chains, 3 treble crochets) into corner chain space **, (make 2 chains, work 3 treble crochets into next chain space) 7 times, make 2 chains, repeat from * twice more, then * to ** once (make 2 chains, work 3 treble crochets into next chain space) 3 times, make 2 chains, join with a slip stitch.

Round 10: Make 5 chains (this counts as 1 treble crochet and 2 chains), work (3 treble crochets into next chain space, make 2 chains) 4 times, * (work 3 treble crochets, 3 chains, 3 treble crochets) into corner chain space **, (make 2 chains, work 3 treble crochets into next chain space) 8 times, make 2 chains, repeat from * twice more, then from * to ** once, (make 2 chains, work 3 treble crochets into next chain space) 3 times, make 2 chains, work 2 treble crochets into next chain space, join with a slip stitch into third of 5 chains. Slip stitch into next chain space.

Change to yarn B
Round 11: Make 3 chains (this counts as a treble crochet), work 2 treble crochets into same chain space, (make 2 chains, work 3 treble crochets into next chain space) 4 times, make 2 chains, * (work 3 treble crochets, 3 chains, 3 treble crochets) into

corner chain space **, (make 2 chains, work 3 treble crochets into next chain space) 9 times, make 2 chains, repeat from * twice more, then from * to ** once (make 2 chains, work 3 treble crochets into next chain space) 4 times, make 2 chains, join with a slip stitch.

Round 12: Make 5 chains (this counts as 1 treble and 2 chains), work (3 treble crochets into next chain space, make 2 chains) 5 times, * (work 3 treble crochets, 3 chains, 3 treble crochets) into corner chain space **, (make 2 chains, work 3 treble crochets into next chain space) 10 times, make 2 chains, repeat from * twice more, then from * to ** once (make 2 chains, work 3 treble crochets into next chain space) 4 times, make 2 chains, work 2 treble crochets into next chain space, join with a slip stitch into third of 5 chains. Slip stitch into next chain space.

Round 13: Make 3 chains (this counts as a treble crochet), work 2 treble crochets into same chain space, (make 2 chains, work 3 treble crochets into next chain space) 5 times, make 2 chains, * (work 3 treble crochets, 3 chains, 3 treble crochets into corner chain space) **, (make 2 chains, work 3 treble crochets into next chain space) 11 times, make 2 chains, repeat from * twice more, then from * to ** once (make 2 chains, work 3 treble crochets into next chain space) 5 times, make 2 chains, join with a slip stitch into top of chain.

Round 14: Make 5 chains (this counts as 1 treble crochet and 2 chains), work (3 treble crochets into next chain space, make 2 chains) 6 times, * (work 3 treble crochets, 3 chains, 3 treble crochets) into corner chain space **, (make 2 chains, work 3 treble crochet into next chain space) 12 times, make 2 chains, repeat from * twice more, then from * to ** once, (make 2 chains, work 3 treble crochets into next chain space) 5 times, make 2 chains, work 2 treble crochets into next chain space, join with a slip stitch into third of 5 chains. Slip stitch into next chain space.

Round 15: Make 3 chains (this counts as a treble crochet), work 2 treble crochets into same chain space, (make 2 chains, work 3 treble crochets into next chain space) 6 times, make 2 chains, * (work 3 treble crochets, 3 chains, 3 treble crochets into corner chain space) **, (make 2 chains, work 3 treble crochets into next chain space) 13 times, make 2 chains, repeat from * twice more, then from * to ** once (make 2 chains, work 3 treble crochets into next chain space) 6 times, make 2 chains, join with a slip stitch into top of chain.

Round 16: Make 1 chain, work 1 double crochet into the top of the chain on the row before, work 1 double crochet into the top of each of the trebles on the previous round, (work 2 double crochets into chain space, work 1 double crochet into the top of next 3 treble crochets) 7 times, * work 3 double crochets into corner chain space, work 1 double crochet into the top of the next 3 treble crochets, (work 2 double crochets into chain space, work 1 double crochet into the top of next 3 treble crochets) 14 times, repeat from * twice more, work 3 double crochets into corner chain space, (work 1 double crochet into top of the next 3 treble crochets, make 2 chains) 7 times, join with a slip stitch.

Fasten off.

HEAD

Using 4mm (US G/6) hook and yarn A make 4 chains, join with a slip stitch into first chain.

Round 1: Make 1 chain, work 6 double crochets into ring, join with a slip stitch.

Round 2: Make 1 chain, work 2 double crochets into each stitch, join with a slip stitch. 12 stitches.

Round 3: Make 1 chain, * work 1 double crochet into the next stitch, work 2 double crochets into following stitch, repeat from * to end. Join with a slip stitch. 18 stitches.

Round 4: Make 1 chain, * work 1 double crochet into the next 2 stitches, work 2 double crochets into following stitch, repeat from * to end. Join with a slip stitch. 24 stitches.

Round 5: Make 1 chain, * work 1 double crochet into the next 3 stitches, work 2 double crochets into following stitch, repeat from * to end. Join with a slip stitch. 30 stitches.

Round 6: Make 1 chain, * work 1 double crochet into the next 4 stitches, work 2 double crochets into following stitch, repeat from * to end. Join with a slip stitch. 36 stitches.

Round 7: Make 1 chain, * work 1 double crochet into the next 5 stitches, work 2 double crochets into following stitch, repeat from * to end. Join with a slip stitch. 42 stitches.

Round 8: Make 1 chain, * work 1 double crochet into the next 6 stitches, work 2 double crochets into following stitch, repeat from * to end. Join with a slip stitch. 48 stitches.

Rounds 9 – 12: Make 1 chain, work 1 double crochet into each stitch to end of round, joining with a slip stitch.

Round 13: Make 1 chain, * work 1 double crochet into next 6 stitches, work 2 double crochets together, repeat from * to end. Join with a slip stitch. 42 stitches.

Round 14: Make 1 chain, * work 1 double crochet into next 5 stitches, work 2 double crochets together, repeat from * to end. Join with a slip stitch. 36 stitches.

Round 15: Make 1 chain, * work 1 double crochet into next 4 stitches, work 2 double crochets together, repeat from * to end. Join with a slip stitch. 30 stitches.

Start stuffing your head at this point and continue to stuff as you decrease.

Round 16: Make 1 chain, * work 1 double crochet into next 3 stitches, work 2 double crochets together, repeat from * to end. Join with a slip stitch. 24 stitches.

Round 17: Make 1 chain, * work 1 double crochet into next 2 stitches, work 2 double crochets together, repeat from * to end. Join with a slip stitch. 18 stitches.

Round 18: Make 1 chain, * work 1 double crochet into next stitch, work 2 double crochets together, repeat from * to end. Join with a slip stitch. 12 stitches.

Round 19: Make 1 chain, work 2 double crochets together to end. Join with a slip stitch. 6 stitches.

Cut yarn, leaving a length long enough for sewing up.

Using a tapestry needle, thread yarn and insert into each stitch, pull tight and secure.

EARS – (MAKE 2)

Using 4mm (US G/6) hook and yarn A, make 5 chains.

Row 1: Work 1 double crochet into second stitch from hook, work 1 double crochet into each stitch to end. 4 stitches.

Row 2: Make 1 chain, work 1 double crochet into each stitch to end.

Row 3: Make 1 chain, work 1 double crochet into next stitch, work 2 double crochets together, work 1 double crochet into last stitch. 3 stitches.

Row 4: Make 1 chain, work 3 double crochets together. 1 stitch.

Fasten off.

MAKING UP

Press as described on page 17. Using photo as a guide, attach ears to side of the bear's head. Using a tapestry needle and embroidery thread, work a nose and 2 eyes onto the face. Attach bear's head to centre of the blanket.

CLOUD COT TOY

Using a super-soft cotton yarn, these clouds are worked flat then stuffed and joined with a double crochet seam once folded in half. This is an easy project to complete in an evening. I used a light weight yarn, but a thicker yarn will make even bigger clouds! I have used plastic links to hang the clouds from the side of a cot.

SKILL LEVEL: SOME EXPERIENCE

YOU'LL NEED:

YARN
1 x 50g of Rowan Summerlite DK or any
No.3 light weight yarn
(photographed in Plaster 452, Seashell 466
and Silvery Blue 468)

HOOK
3.5mm (US E/4) hook

EXTRAS
Toy stuffing

CLOUD COT TOY

SIZE
19cm/7½in long and 6cm/2¼in high (excluding tie)

TENSION
23 sts and 26 rows to 10cm/4in
Measured over double crochet using 3.5mm (US E/4) hook.

CLOUDS – (MAKE 3)
Using 3.5mm (US E/4) hook, make 11 chains.

Row 1: Work 1 double crochet into the second stitch from the hook, work 1 double crochet into each stitch to end. 10 stitches.

Row 2: Make 1 chain, work 2 double crochets into the next stitch, work 1 double crochet into next 8 stitches, work 2 double crochets into the next stitch. 12 stitches.

Row 3: Make 1 chain, work 2 double crochets into the next stitch, work 1 double crochet into next 10 stitches, work 2 double crochets into the next stitch. 14 stitches.

Row 4: Make 1 chain, work 2 double crochets into the next stitch, work 1 double crochet into next 12 stitches, work 2 double crochets into the next stitch. 16 stitches.

Rows 5 – 7: Make 1 chain, work 1 double crochet into the next 16 stitches.

Row 8: Make 1 chain, work 2 double crochets into the next stitch, work 1 double crochet into next 14 stitches, work 2 double crochets into the next stitch. 18 stitches.

Row 9: Make 1 chain, work 2 double crochets into the next stitch, work 1 double crochet into next 16 stitches, work 2 double crochets into the next stitch. 20 stitches.

Row 10: Make 1 chain, work 2 double crochets into the next stitch, work 1 double crochet into next 18 stitches, work 2 double crochets into the next stitch. 22 stitches.

Rows 11 – 16: Make 1 chain, work 1 double crochet into the next 22 stitches.

Row 17: Make 1 chain, work 2 double crochets into the next stitch, work 1 double crochet into next 20 stitches, work 2 double crochets into the next stitch. 24 stitches.

Row 18: Make 1 chain, work 2 double crochets into the next stitch, work 1 double crochet into next 22 stitches, work 2 double crochets into the next stitch. 26 stitches.

Row 19: Make 1 chain, work 2 double crochets into the next stitch, work 1 double crochet into next 24 stitches, work 2 double crochets into the next stitch. 28 stitches.

Row 20: Make 1 chain, work 2 double crochets into the next stitch, work 1 double crochet into next 26 stitches, work 2 double crochets into the next stitch. 30 stitches.

Row 21: Make 1 chain, work 2 double crochets into the next stitch, work 1 double crochet into next 28 stitches, work 2 double crochets into the next stitch. 32 stitches.

Row 22: Make 1 chain, work 2 double crochets into the next stitch, work 1 double crochet into next 30 stitches, work 2 double crochets into the next stitch. 34 stitches.

Rows 23 – 27: Make 1 chain, work 1 double crochet into the next 34 stitches.

Row 28: Make 1 chain, work 2 double crochets together, work 1 double crochet into the next 30 stitches, work 2 double crochets together. 32 stitches.

Row 29: Make 1 chain, work 2 double crochets together, work 1 double crochet into the next 28 stitches, work 2 double crochets together. 30 stitches.

Row 30: Make 1 chain, work 2 double crochets together, work 1 double crochet into the next 26 stitches, work 2 double crochets together. 28 stitches.

Row 31: Make 1 chain, work 2 double crochets together, work 1 double crochet into the next 24 stitches, work 2 double crochets together. 26 stitches.

Row 32: Make 1 chain, work 2 double crochets together, work 1 double crochet into the next 22 stitches, work 2 double crochets together. 24 stitches.

Row 33: Make 1 chain, work 2 double crochets together, work 1 double crochet into the next 20 stitches, work 2 double crochets together. 22 stitches.

Row 34: Make 1 chain, work 2 double crochets together, work 1 double crochet into the next 18 stitches, work 2 double crochets together. 20 stitches.

Rows 35 – 38: Make 1 chain, work 1 double crochet into next 20 stitches.

Row 39: Make 1 chain, work 2 double crochets together, work 1 double crochet into the next 16 stitches, work 2 double crochets together. 18 stitches.

Row 40: Make 1 chain, work 2 double crochets together, work 1 double crochet into the next 14 stitches, work 2 double crochets together. 16 stitches.

Row 41: Make 1 chain, work 2 double crochets together, work 1 double crochet into the next 12 stitches, work 2 double crochets together. 14 stitches.

Row 42: Make 1 chain, work 2 double crochets together, work 1 double crochet into the next 10 stitches, work 2 double crochets together. 12 stitches.

Row 43: Make 1 chain, work 2 double crochets together, work 1 double crochet into the next 8 stitches, work 2 double crochets together. 10 stitches.

Row 44: Make 1 chain, work 2 double crochets together, work 1 double crochet into the next 6 stitches, work 2 double crochets together. 8 stitches.

Fasten off.

MAKING UP

Press as described on page 17.
Fold cloud in half, insert hook and rejoin yarn, work 50 double crochets along side edge to join, stuffing as you go.
Fasten off.

TIE

Using 3.5mm (US E/4) hook, make 8 chains, join with a slip stitch into first chain made. Make 1 chain, work 1 double crochet into each stitch until tie measures 12cm/4¾in, join with a slip stitch and fasten off.
Attach to the back of cloud just behind the highest ridge.

I used child-safe plastic link rings to attach.

STAR MOBILE

A modern star to keep your child entertained while on the move. Worked in Rowan Handknit Cotton, this star will be durable and safe if chewed on. Using the strap to attach to a plastic link, this star can easily be moved from car seat to pram. You could even put a rattle inside the star before sewing it up.

SKILL LEVEL: SOME EXPERIENCE

YOU'LL NEED:

YARN
1 x 50g of Rowan Handknit Cotton or any
No.4 medium weight yarn
(photographed in Cloud 345)

HOOK
4.5mm (US 7) hook

EXTRAS
Toy stuffing
Stitch markers

STAR MOBILE

SIZE

19cm/7½in high and 19cm/7½in wide (excluding tie)

TENSION

18 sts and 21 rows to 10cm/4in
Measured over double crochet using 4.5mm (US 7) hook.

STAR POINTS – (MAKE 5)

Using 4.5mm (US 7) hook make a magic loop and work 4 double crochets into loop.

Round 1: * Work 1 double crochet into the next stitch, work 2 double crochets into the following stitch, repeat from * once more. 6 stitches.

Round 2: * Work 1 double crochet into the next 2 stitches, work 2 double crochets into the following stitch, repeat from * once more. 8 stitches.

Round 3: * Work 1 double crochet into the next 3 stitches, work 2 double crochets into the following stitch, repeat from * once more. 10 stitches.

Round 4: * Work 1 double crochet into the next 4 stitches, work 2 double crochets into the following stitch, repeat from * once more. 12 stitches.

Round 5: * Work 1 double crochet into the next 5 stitches, work 2 double crochets into the following stitch, repeat from * once more. 14 stitches.

Round 6: * Work 1 double crochet into the next 6 stitches, work 2 double crochets into the following stitch, repeat from * once more. 16 stitches.

Round 7: * Work 1 double crochet into the next 7 stitches, work 2 double crochets into the following stitch, repeat from * once more. 18 stitches.

Round 8: * Work 1 double crochet into the next 8 stitches, work 2 double crochets into the following stitch, repeat from * once more. 20 stitches.

Round 9: * Work 1 double crochet into the next 9 stitches, work 2 double crochets into the following stitch, repeat from * once more. 22 stitches.

Round 10: * Work 1 double crochet into the next 10 stitches, work 2 double crochets into the following stitch, repeat from * once more. 24 stitches.

Round 11: * Work 1 double crochet into the next 24 stitches.

Work a slip stitch into the next stitch and fasten off.

Stuff the star points.

STAR CENTRE

Using 4.5mm (US 7) hook insert hook in stitch next to slip stitch, rejoin yarn.

Make 1 chain, work 1 double crochet into the same stitch as the chain, work 1 double crochet into the next 9 stitches. Place a stitch marker on the next stitch.

Repeat last step for 4 remaining points. 45 stitches.

Next Round: * Work 1 double crochet into next 7 stitches, double crochet 2 stitches together, repeat from * to end. 40 stitches.

Next Round: * Work 1 double crochet into next 6 stitches, double crochet 2 stitches together, repeat from * to end. 35 stitches.

Next Round: * Work 1 double crochet into next 5 stitches, double crochet 2 stitches together, repeat from * to end. 30 stitches.

Next Round: * Work 1 double crochet into next 4 stitches, double crochet 2 stitches together, repeat from * to end. 25 stitches.

Next Round: * Work 1 double crochet into next 3 stitches, double crochet 2 stitches together, repeat from * to end. 20 stitches.

Next Round: * Work 1 double crochet into next 2 stitches, double crochet 2 stitches together, repeat from * to end. 15 stitches.

Next Round: * Work 1 double crochet into next stitch, double crochet 2 stitches together, repeat from * to end. 10 stitches.

Next Round: * Double crochet 2 stitches together, repeat from * to end. 5 stitches.

Cut a tail long enough to sew up.

To join the seams between the star points, with right sides of star points together, rejoin yarn going through both stitches on each star point, work 1 double crochet into next 3 stitches.

Thread yarn with tail end of yarn, using a running stitch through the top of the stitches, pull to secure.

Using 4.5mm (US 7) hook insert hook into second stitch from stitch marker, rejoin yarn and work to match first side, stuffing as you go.

MAKING UP
TIE

Using 4.5mm (US 7) hook, make 5 chains, join with a slip stitch into first chain made. Make 1 chain, work 1 double crochet into each stitch until tie measures 10cm/4in, join with a slip stitch and fasten off. Attach tie to the back of one of the star points with mattress stitch; this will be the top of your star.

TEDDY BEAR

This beautiful bear in a simple two-colour design is a great statement piece to use up any of your chunkier yarns. With his striking bow tie, which can be made in any colour of your choice, this lovable teddy bear is sure to be a favourite.

SKILL LEVEL: SOME EXPERIENCE

YOU'LL NEED:

YARN
Rowan Cotton Glace or any No.3
light weight yarn
A – 2 x 50g of Dawn Grey 831
B – 1 x 50g of Ivy 812
C – 1 x 50g of Black 727

HOOK
3.5mm (US E/4) hook

EXTRAS
Toy stuffing
2 x Black safety eyes
Black triangle nose
Stitch marker

TEDDY BEAR

SIZE
17cm/6½in high

TENSION
24 sts and 26 rows to 10cm/4in
Measured over double crochet using 3.5mm (US E/4) hook.

HEAD
Using 3.5mm (US E/4) hook and yarn A make a magic ring.
Round 1: Work 6 double crochets into the ring. 6 stitches.
Round 2: * Work 2 double crochets into next stitch, repeat from * to end. 12 stitches.
Round 3: * Work 1 double crochet into next stitch, work 2 double crochets into next stitch, repeat from * to end. 18 stitches.
Round 4: * Work 1 double crochet into next 2 stitches, work 2 double crochets into next stitch, repeat from * to end. 24 stitches.
Round 5: * Work 1 double crochet into next 3 stitches, work 2 double crochets into next stitch, repeat from * to end. 30 stitches.
Round 6: * Work 1 double crochet into next 4 stitches, work 2 double crochets into next stitch, repeat from * to end. 36 stitches.
Round 7: * Work 1 double crochet into next 5 stitches, work 2 double crochets into next stitch, repeat from * to end. 42 stitches.
Round 8: * Work 1 double crochet into next 6 stitches, work 2 double crochets into next stitch, repeat from * to end. 48 stitches.
Round 9: Work 1 double crochet into each stitch.
Rounds 10 – 18: As round 9.
Attach safety eyes between rounds 13 and 14 with 8 stitches between them.
Round 19: * Work 1 double crochet into next 6 stitches, work 2 double crochets together, repeat from * to end. 42 stitches.
Round 20: * Work 1 double crochet into next 5 stitches, work 2 double crochets together, repeat from * to end. 36 stitches.

Round 21: * Work 1 double crochet into next 4 stitches, work 2 double crochets together, repeat from * to end. 30 stitches.

Round 22: * Work 1 double crochet into next 3 stitches, work 2 double crochets together, repeat from * to end. 24 stitches. Start to stuff and continue stuffing as you work.

Round 23: * Work 1 double crochet into next 2 stitches, work 2 double crochets together, repeat from * to end. 18 stitches.

Round 24: * Work 1 double crochet into next stitch, work 2 double crochets together, repeat from * to end. 12 stitches.

Round 25: * Work 2 double crochets together, repeat from * to end. 6 stitches.
Fasten off leaving a long length of yarn. Sew a running stitch around last round, pull tight to secure and close hole.

MUZZLE

Using 3.5mm (US E/4) hook and yarn A make a magic ring.

Round 1: Work 6 double crochets into the ring. 6 stitches.

Round 2: * Work 2 double crochets into next stitch, repeat from * to end. 12 stitches.

Round 3: * Work 1 double crochet into next stitch, work 2 double crochets into next stitch, repeat from * to end. 18 stitches.

Round 4: Work 1 double crochet into each stitch.

Rounds 5 – 6: As round 4.
Fasten off leaving a long length of yarn.

EARS – (MAKE 2)

Using 3.5mm (US E/4) hook and yarn A make a magic ring.

Round 1: Work 6 double crochets into the ring. 6 stitches.

Round 2: * Work 2 double crochets into next stitch, repeat from * to end. 12 stitches.

Round 3: * Work 1 double crochet into next stitch, work 2 double crochets into next stitch, repeat from * to end. 18 stitches.

Round 4: Work 1 double crochet into each stitch.

Round 5: As round 4.

Round 6: * Work 1 double crochet into next stitch, work 2 double crochets together, repeat from * to end. 12 stitches.
Fasten off leaving a long length of yarn.

BODY

Using 3.5mm (US E/4) hook and yarn A make a magic ring.

Round 1: Work 6 double crochets into the ring. 6 stitches.

Round 2: * Work 2 double crochets into next stitch, repeat from * to end. 12 stitches.

Round 3: * Work 1 double crochet into next stitch, work 2 double crochets into next stitch, repeat from * to end. 18 stitches.

Round 4: * Work 1 double crochet into next 2 stitches, work 2 double crochets into next stitch, repeat from * to end. 24 stitches.

Round 5: * Work 1 double crochet into next 3 stitches, work 2 double crochets into next stitch, repeat from * to end. 30 stitches.

Round 6: * Work 1 double crochet into next 4 stitches, work 2 double crochets into next stitch, repeat from * to end. 36 stitches.

Round 7: * Work 1 double crochet into next 5 stitches, work 2 double crochets into next stitch, repeat from * to end. 42 stitches.

Round 8: * Work 1 double crochet into next 6 stitches, work 2 double crochets into next stitch, repeat from * to end. 48 stitches.

Round 9: * Work 1 double crochet into next 7 stitches, work 2 double crochets into next stitch, repeat from * to end. 54 stitches.

Round 10: Work 1 double crochet into each stitch.

Rounds 11 – 21: As round 10.

Round 22: * Work 1 double crochet into next 7 stitches, work 2 double crochets

together, repeat from * to end. 48 stitches.

Round 23: As round 10.

Round 24: * Work 1 double crochet into next 6 stitches, work 2 double crochets together, repeat from * to end. 42 stitches.

Round 25: As round 10.

Round 26: * Work 1 double crochet into next 5 stitches, work 2 double crochets together, repeat from * to end. 36 stitches.

Round 27: As round 10.

Round 28: * Work 1 double crochet into next 4 stitches, work 2 double crochets together, repeat from * to end. 30 stitches.

Round 29: As round 10.

Round 30: * Work 1 double crochet into next 3 stitches, work 2 double crochets together, repeat from * to end. 24 stitches.

Round 31: As round 10.

Round 32: * Work 1 double crochet into next 2 stitches, work 2 double crochets together, repeat from * to end. 18 stitches.

Rounds 33 – 34: As round 10.

Fasten off leaving a long length of yarn.

ARMS – (MAKE 2)

Using 3.5mm (US E/4) hook and yarn A make a magic ring.

Round 1: Work 4 double crochets into the ring. 4 stitches.

Round 2: * Work 2 double crochets into next stitch, repeat from * to end. 8 stitches.

Round 3: * Work 1 double crochet into next stitch, work 2 double crochets into next stitch, repeat from * to end. 12 stitches.

Round 4: Work 1 double crochet into each stitch.

Round 5: As round 3.

Round 6: * Work 1 double crochet into next stitch, work 2 double crochets together, repeat from * to end. 8 stitches.

Rounds 7 – 24: As round 4.

Fasten off leaving a long length of yarn.

LEGS – (MAKE 2)

Using 3.5mm (US E/4) hook and yarn A make a magic ring.

Round 1: Work 6 double crochets into the ring. 6 stitches.

Round 2: * Work 2 double crochets into next stitch, repeat from * to end. 12 stitches.

Round 3: * Work 1 double crochet into next stitch, work 2 double crochets into next stitch, repeat from * to end. 18 stitches.

Round 4: Work 1 double crochet into each stitch.

Round 5: As round 4.

Round 6: Work 1 double crochet into next 5 stitches, (work 2 double crochets together) 4 times, work 1 double crochet into next 5 stitches. 14 stitches.

Round 7: Work 1 double crochet into next 5 stitches, (work 2 double crochets together) twice, work 1 double crochet into next 5 stitches. 12 stitches.

Rounds 8 – 21: As round 4.

Fasten off leaving a long length of yarn.

TAIL

Using 3.5mm (US E/4) hook and yarn A make a magic ring.

Round 1: Work 6 double crochets into the ring. 6 stitches.

Round 2: * Work 2 double crochets into next stitch, repeat from * to end. 12 stitches.

Round 3: Work 1 double crochet into each stitch.

Rounds 4 – 5: As round 3.

Fasten off leaving a long length of yarn.

BOW TIE

Using 3.5mm (US E/4) hook and yarn A make 25 chains.

Row 1: Work 1 double crochet into second chain from hook, work 1 double crochet into each stitch, turn. 24 stitches.

Row 2: Make 1 chain, work 1 double crochet into each stitch, turn.

Rows 3 – 5: As row 2.

Row 6: Make 1 chain, work 1 double crochet into each stitch, **do not turn**.

Fold in half and slip stitch last row to starting chain.

Fasten off leaving a long length of yarn. Turn bow section so that stitches lie on the back of the bow.

STRAP

Using 3.5mm (US E/4) hook and yarn A make 9 chains.

Row 1: Work 1 double crochet into second chain from hook, work 1 double crochet into each stitch, turn. 8 stitches.

Row 2: Make 1 chain, work 1 double crochet into each stitch, turn.

Wrap strap around bow and slip stitch edges together around bow.

Fasten off leaving a long length of yarn.

MAKING UP

Attach nose to centre of muzzle, sew muzzle to head between eyes. Stuff body, sew head to body. Sew ears to side of head. Sew arms to body. Stuff legs leaving last 2 rounds unstuffed, sew legs in sitting position to lower part of body. Sew bow tie to neck. Sew tail to base of body, stuffing as you work.

BUNNY RABBIT

This bunny rabbit is the perfect gift for your child, with its easy-to-construct features and dress that can be made in different shades. Why not make a whole family of bunny rabbits in a variety of colours and sizes?

SKILL LEVEL: SOME EXPERIENCE

YOU'LL NEED:

YARN
Rowan Handknit Cotton or any No.3
light weight yarn
A – 1 x 50g of Sea Foam 352
B – 1 x 50g of Ecru 251
C – 1 x 50g of Black 252

HOOK
4mm (US G/6) hook

EXTRAS
Toy stuffing
2 x Black safety eyes
1 x Black triangle nose
Stitch marker

BUNNY RABBIT

SIZE

Approximately 35cm/13¾in tall

TENSION

18 sts and 20 rows to 10cm/4in
Measured over double crochet using 4mm
(US G/6) hook.

HEAD

Using 4mm (US G/6) hook and yarn B make
a magic ring.

Round 1: Work 6 double crochets into the
ring. 6 stitches.

Round 2: * Work 2 double crochets into
next stitch, repeat from * to end. 12 stitches.

Round 3: * Work 1 double crochet into next
stitch, work 2 double crochets into next
stitch, repeat from * to end. 18 stitches.

Round 4: * Work 1 double crochet into next
2 stitches, work 2 double crochets into next
stitch, repeat from * to end. 24 stitches.

Round 5: * Work 1 double crochet into next
3 stitches, work 2 double crochets into next
stitch, repeat from * to end. 30 stitches.

Round 6: * Work 1 double crochet into next
4 stitches, work 2 double crochets into next
stitch, repeat from * to end. 36 stitches.

Round 7: Work 1 double crochet into
each stitch.

Rounds 8 – 16: As round 7.

Attach safety eyes between rounds 11 and
12 with 6 stitches between them.

Attach nose between rounds 13 and 14,
centrally between eyes.

Round 17: * Work 1 double crochet into
next 4 stitches, work 2 double crochets
together, repeat from * to end. 30 stitches.

Round 18: * Work 1 double crochet into
next 3 stitches, work 2 double crochets
together, repeat from * to end. 24 stitches.

Start to stuff and continue stuffing as
you work.

Round 19: * Work 1 double crochet into
next 2 stitches, work 2 double crochets

together, repeat from * to end. 18 stitches.

Round 20: * Work 1 double crochet into next stitch, work 2 double crochets together, repeat from * to end. 12 stitches.

Round 21: * Work 2 double crochets together, repeat from * to end. 6 stitches. Fasten off leaving a long length of yarn. Sew a running stitch around last round, pull tight to secure and close hole.

EARS – (MAKE 2)

Using 4mm (US G/6) hook and yarn B make a magic ring.

Round 1: Work 4 double crochets into the ring. 4 stitches.

Round 2: Work 1 double crochet into each stitch.

Round 3: * Work 1 double crochet into next stitch, work 2 double crochets into next stitch, repeat from * to end. 6 stitches.

Round 4: * Work 1 double crochet into next 2 stitches, work 2 double crochets into next stitch, repeat from * to end. 8 stitches.

Round 5: * Work 1 double crochet into next 3 stitches, work 2 double crochets into next stitch, repeat from * to end. 10 stitches.

Round 6: * Work 1 double crochet into next 4 stitches, work 2 double crochets into next stitch, repeat from * to end. 12 stitches.

Round 7: * Work 1 double crochet into next 5 stitches, work 2 double crochets into next stitch, repeat from * to end. 14 stitches.

Rounds 8 – 17: As round 2.
Fasten off leaving a long length of yarn.

BODY

Using 4mm (US G/6) hook and yarn B make a magic ring.

Round 1: Work 6 double crochets into the ring. 6 stitches.

Round 2: * Work 2 double crochets into

next stitch, repeat from * to end. 12 stitches.

Round 3: * Work 1 double crochet into next stitch, work 2 double crochets into next stitch, repeat from * to end. 18 stitches.

Round 4: * Work 1 double crochet into next 2 stitches, work 2 double crochets into next stitch, repeat from * to end. 24 stitches.

Round 5: * Work 1 double crochet into next 3 stitches, work 2 double crochets into next stitch, repeat from * to end. 30 stitches.

Round 6: * Work 1 double crochet into next 4 stitches, work 2 double crochets into next stitch, repeat from * to end. 36 stitches.

Round 7: Work 1 double crochet into each stitch.

Rounds 8 – 20: As round 7.

Round 21: * Work 1 double crochet into next 4 stitches, work 2 double crochets together, repeat from * to end. 30 stitches.

Round 22: As round 7.

Round 23: * Work 1 double crochet into next 3 stitches, work 2 double crochets together, repeat from * to end. 24 stitches.

Round 24: As round 7.

Round 25: * Work 1 double crochet into next 2 stitches, work 2 double crochets together, repeat from * to end. 18 stitches.

Round 26: As round 7.

Round 27: * Work 1 double crochet into next stitch, work 2 double crochets together, repeat from * to end. 12 stitches.

Rounds 28 – 29: As round 7.
Fasten off leaving a long length of yarn.

DRESS – WORKED ONTO BODY FROM NECK DOWNWARDS

Using 4mm (US G/6) hook join yarn A to last round of body.

Round 1: Working into back loop only, work a round of double crochet around neck of body.

Round 2: * Work 1 double crochet into next stitch, work 2 double crochets into next stitch, repeat from * to end. 18 stitches.

Round 3: * Work 1 double crochet into next 2 stitches, work 2 double crochets into next stitch, repeat from * to end. 24 stitches.

Round 4: Work 1 double crochet into each stitch.

Round 5: * Work 1 double crochet into next 3 stitches, work 2 double crochets into next stitch, repeat from * to end. 30 stitches.

Round 6: As round 4.

Round 7: * Work 1 double crochet into next 4 stitches, work 2 double crochets into next stitch, repeat from * to end. 36 stitches.

Round 8: As round 4.

Round 9: * Work 1 double crochet into next 5 stitches, work 2 double crochets into next stitch, repeat from * to end. 42 stitches.

Round 10: As round 4.

Round 11: * Work 1 double crochet into next 6 stitches, work 2 double crochets into next stitch, repeat from * to end. 48 stitches.

Rounds 12 – 13: As round 4.

Round 14: * Work 1 double crochet into next 7 stitches, work 2 double crochets into next stitch, repeat from * to end. 54 stitches.

Rounds 15 – 16: As round 4.

Round 17: * Work 1 double crochet into next 8 stitches, work 2 double crochets into next stitch, repeat from * to end. 60 stitches.

Rounds 18 – 20: As round 4.

Round 21: * Work 1 double crochet into next 9 stitches, work 2 double crochets into next stitch, repeat from * to end. 66 stitches.

Rounds 22 – 24: As round 4.

Round 25: * Work 1 double crochet into next 10 stitches, work 2 double crochets into next stitch, repeat from * to end. 72 stitches.

Rounds 26 – 27: As round 4.

Round 28: Work 1 double crochet into each stitch, join with a slip stitch to start of round. Fasten off leaving a long length of yarn.

LEGS – (MAKE 2)

Using 4mm (US G/6) hook and yarn B make a magic ring.

Round 1: Work 4 double crochets into the ring. 4 stitches.

Round 2: * Work 2 double crochets into next stitch, repeat from * to end. 8 stitches.

Round 3: Work 1 double crochet into each stitch.

Start to stuff and continue stuffing as you work, up to last 4 rounds.

Rounds 4 – 24: As round 3.

Fasten off leaving a long length of yarn.
Leave last 4 rounds unstuffed.

ARMS – (MAKE 2)

Using 4mm (US G/6) hook and yarn B make a magic ring.

Round 1: Work 6 double crochets into the ring. 6 stitches.

Round 2: * Work 2 double crochets into next stitch, repeat from * to end. 12 stitches.

Round 3: Work 1 double crochet into each stitch.

Rounds 4 – 5: As round 3.

Stuff last 5 rounds only.

Round 6: * Work 1 double crochet into next stitch, work 2 double crochets together, repeat from * to end. 8 stitches.

Rounds 7 – 18: As round 3.

Change to yarn A.

Rounds 19 – 22: As round 3.

Fasten off leaving a long length of yarn.

MAKING UP

Use yarn C to embroider mouth 4 rounds below nose. Fold ears in half, sew together, then sew to top of head. Attach arms to side of body. Attach legs to bottom of body.

OCTOPUS

These octopuses will bring the magic of the ocean to any toy box. Their cute smiles, rosy cheeks and beady eyes will really appeal to young children. Customize them by adding the bow detail in different places, and making them in contrasting colours.

SKILL LEVEL: SOME EXPERIENCE

YOU'LL NEED:

YARN

Rowan Handknit Cotton or any No.3
light weight yarn

For the pink octopus
A – 2 x 50g of Sugar 303
B – 1 x 50g of Raspberry 356
C – 1 x 50g of Ballet Pink 372
D – 1 x 50g of Black 252

For the blue octopus
A – 2 x 50g of Cloud 345
B – 1 x 50g of Atlantic 346
C – 1 x 50g of Ballet Pink 372
D – 1 x 50g of Black 252

HOOK

4mm (US G/6) hook

EXTRAS

Toy stuffing
2 x Black safety eyes
Stitch marker

OCTOPUS

SIZE

21cm/8¼in from head to end of tentacles

TENSION

18 sts and 20 rows to 10cm/4in
Measured over double crochet using 4mm
(US G/6) hook.

LEGS – (MAKE 8)

Using 4mm (US G/6) hook and yarn A make
a magic ring.

Round 1: Work 4 double crochets into the
ring. 4 stitches.

Round 2: * Work 2 double crochets into
next stitch, repeat from * to end. 8 stitches.

Round 3: Work 1 double crochet into each
stitch.

Start to stuff and continue as you work.

Rounds 4 – 24: As round 3.

Fasten off leaving a long length of yarn.

BODY AND HEAD

Using 4mm (US G/6) hook and yarn A make
a magic ring.

Round 1: Work 6 double crochets into the
ring. 6 stitches.

Round 2: * Work 2 double crochets into
next stitch, repeat from * to end. 12 stitches.

Round 3: * Work 1 double crochet into next
stitch, work 2 double crochets into next
stitch, repeat from * to end. 18 stitches.

Round 4: * Work 1 double crochet into next
2 stitches, work 2 double crochets into next
stitch, repeat from * to end. 24 stitches.

Round 5: * Work 1 double crochet into next
3 stitches, work 2 double crochets into next
stitch, repeat from * to end. 30 stitches.

Round 6: * Work 1 double crochet into next
4 stitches, work 2 double crochets into next
stitch, repeat from * to end. 36 stitches.

Round 7: * Work 1 double crochet into next
5 stitches, work 2 double crochets into next
stitch, repeat from * to end. 42 stitches.

Round 8: * Work 1 double crochet into next 6 stitches, work 2 double crochets into next stitch, repeat from * to end. 48 stitches.

Round 9: Work 1 double crochet into each stitch.

Rounds 10 – 22: As round 9.

Round 23: * Work 1 double crochet into next 6 stitches, work 2 double crochets together, repeat from * to end. 42 stitches.

Round 24: * Work 1 double crochet into next 5 stitches, work 2 double crochets together, repeat from * to end. 36 stitches.

Round 25: * Work 1 double crochet into next 7 stitches, work 2 double crochets together, repeat from * to end. 32 stitches.

Rounds 26 – 29: As round 9.

Fasten off leaving a long length of yarn.

CHEEKS – (MAKE 2)

Using 4mm (US G/6) hook and yarn C make a magic ring.

Round 1: Work 4 double crochets into the ring. 4 stitches.

Fasten off leaving a long length of yarn.

BOW

Using 4mm (US G/6) hook and yarn A make 25 chains.

Row 1: Work 1 double crochet into second chain from hook, work 1 double crochet into each stitch, turn. 24 stitches.

Row 2: Make 1 chain, work 1 double crochet into each stitch, turn.

Rows 3 – 5: As row 2.

Row 6: Make 1 chain, work 1 double crochet into each stitch, **do not turn**.

Fold in half and slip stitch last row to starting chain.

Fasten off leaving a long length of yarn. Turn bow section so that stitches lie on the back of the bow.

STRAP

Using 4mm (US G/6) hook and yarn A make 9 chains.

Row 1: Work 1 double crochet into second chain from hook, work 1 double crochet into each stitch, turn. 8 stitches.

Row 2: Make 1 chain, work 1 double crochet into each stitch, turn.

Wrap strap around bow and slip stitch edges together around bow.

Fasten off leaving a long length of yarn.

MAKING UP

Sew through front loop only of 4 stitches on each leg around base of body. Attach safety eyes to head between rounds 19 and 20 with 6 stitches between them. Stuff body. Using yarn D embroider a mouth 3 rounds below eyes. Sew cheeks to side of face. For pink octopus, sew bow to top of head; for blue octopus, sew bow under mouth.

BASE

Using 4mm (US G/6) hook and yarn A make a magic ring.

Round 1: Work 6 double crochets into the ring. 6 stitches.

Round 2: Work 2 double crochets into each stitch. 12 stitches.

Round 3: * Work 1 double crochet into next stitch, work 2 double crochets into next stitch, repeat from * to end. 18 stitches.

Round 4: * Work 1 double crochet into next 2 stitches, work 2 double crochets into next stitch, repeat from * to end. 24 stitches.

Round 5: * Work 1 double crochet into next 3 stitches, work 2 double crochets into next stitch, repeat from * to end. 30 stitches.

Round 6: * Work 1 double crochet into next 14 stitches, work 2 double crochets into next stitch, repeat from * to end. 32 stitches.

Fasten off leaving a long length of yarn.

Sew base to body through legs.

GIRAFFE

This curious giraffe sits tall and proud. Customize your giraffe by going for a different colour option or stick to more traditional animal colourings. Keep your giraffe warm with a personalized coloured scarf.

SKILL LEVEL: SOME EXPERIENCE

YOU'LL NEED:

YARN
Rowan Summerlite DK or any No.3
light weight yarn
A – 2 x 50g of Summer 453
B – 1 x 50g of Khaki 461
C – 1 x 50g of Cantaloupe 456
D – 1 x 50g of Rouge 462

HOOK
4mm (US G/6) hook

EXTRAS
Toy stuffing
2 x Black safety eyes
Stitch marker

GIRAFFE

SIZE
21cm/8¾in high

TENSION
22 sts and 24 rows to 10cm/4in
Measured over double crochet using 4mm
(US G/6) hook.

HEAD
Using 4mm (US G/6) hook and yarn A make
a magic ring.

Round 1: Work 6 double crochets into the
ring. 6 stitches.

Round 2: * Work 2 double crochets into
next stitch, repeat from * to end. 12 stitches.

Round 3: * Work 1 double crochet into next
stitch, work 2 double crochets into next
stitch, repeat from * to end. 18 stitches.

Round 4: * Work 1 double crochet into next
2 stitches, work 2 double crochets into next
stitch, repeat from * to end. 24 stitches.

Round 5: * Work 1 double crochet into next
3 stitches, work 2 double crochets into next
stitch, repeat from * to end. 30 stitches.

Round 6: * Work 1 double crochet into next
4 stitches, work 2 double crochets into next
stitch, repeat from * to end. 36 stitches.

Round 7: * Work 1 double crochet into next
5 stitches, work 2 double crochets into next
stitch, repeat from * to end. 42 stitches.

Round 8: Work 1 double crochet into
each stitch.

Rounds 9 – 19: As round 8.
Attach safety eyes between rounds 13 and
14 with 7 stitches between them.

Round 20: * Work 1 double crochet into
next 5 stitches, work 2 double crochets
together, repeat from * to end. 36 stitches.

Round 21: * Work 1 double crochet into
next 4 stitches, work 2 double crochets
together, repeat from * to end. 30 stitches.

Round 22: * Work 1 double crochet into
next 3 stitches, work 2 double crochets
together, repeat from * to end. 24 stitches.

Start to stuff and continue stuffing as you work.

Round 23: * Work 1 double crochet into next 2 stitches, work 2 double crochets together, repeat from * to end. 18 stitches.

Round 24: * Work 1 double crochet into next stitch, work 2 double crochets together, repeat from * to end. 12 stitches.

Round 25: * Work 2 double crochets together, repeat from * to end. 6 stitches.
Fasten off leaving a long length of yarn.
Sew a running stitch around last round, pull tight to secure and close hole.

MOUTH

Using 4mm (US G/6) hook and yarn B make a magic ring.

Round 1: Work 6 double crochets into the ring. 6 stitches.

Round 2: * Work 2 double crochets into next stitch, repeat from * to end. 12 stitches.

Round 3: * Work 1 double crochet into next stitch, work 2 double crochets into next stitch, repeat from * to end. 18 stitches.

Round 4: Work 1 double crochet into each stitch.

Rounds 5 – 6: As round 4.
Fasten off leaving a long length of yarn.

HORNS – (MAKE 2)

Using 4mm (US G/6) hook and yarn B make a magic ring.

Round 1: Work 4 double crochets into the ring. 4 stitches.

Round 2: * Work 2 double crochets into next stitch, repeat from * to end. 8 stitches.

Round 3: Work 1 double crochet into each stitch.

Round 4: As round 3.

Round 5: * Work 1 double crochet into next 2 stitches, work 2 double crochets together,

repeat from * to end. 6 stitches.
Change to yarn A.
Start to stuff and continue stuffing as you work.

Rounds 6 – 10: As round 3.
Fasten off leaving a long length of yarn.

EARS – (MAKE 2)

Using 4mm (US G/6) hook and yarn A make a magic ring.

Round 1: Work 4 double crochets into the ring. 4 stitches.

Round 2: Work 1 double crochet into each stitch.

Round 3: * Work 1 double crochet into next stitch, work 2 double crochets into next stitch, repeat from * to end. 6 stitches.

Round 4: * Work 1 double crochet into next 2 stitches, work 2 double crochets into next stitch, repeat from * to end. 8 stitches.

Round 5: * Work 1 double crochet into next 3 stitches, work 2 double crochets into next stitch, repeat from * to end. 10 stitches.

Rounds 6 – 9: As round 2.
Fasten off leaving a long length of yarn.

BODY

Using 4mm (US G/6) hook and yarn A make a magic ring.

Round 1: Work 6 double crochets into the ring. 6 stitches.

Round 2: * Work 2 double crochets into next stitch, repeat from * to end. 12 stitches.

Round 3: * Work 1 double crochet into next stitch, work 2 double crochets into next stitch, repeat from * to end. 18 stitches.

Round 4: * Work 1 double crochet into next 2 stitches, work 2 double crochets into next stitch, repeat from * to end. 24 stitches.

Round 5: * Work 1 double crochet into next 3 stitches, work 2 double crochets into next

stitch, repeat from * to end. 30 stitches.

Round 6: * Work 1 double crochet into next 4 stitches, work 2 double crochets into next stitch, repeat from * to end. 36 stitches.

Round 7: * Work 1 double crochet into next 5 stitches, work 2 double crochets into next stitch, repeat from * to end. 42 stitches.

Round 8: * Work 1 double crochet into next 6 stitches, work 2 double crochets into next stitch, repeat from * to end. 48 stitches.

Round 9: Work 1 double crochet into each stitch.

Rounds 10 – 20: As round 9.

Round 21: * Work 1 double crochet into next 6 stitches, work 2 double crochets together, repeat from * to end. 42 stitches.

Rounds 22 – 23: As round 9.

Round 24: * Work 1 double crochet into next 5 stitches, work 2 double crochets together, repeat from * to end. 36 stitches.

Rounds 25 – 26: As round 9.

Round 27: * Work 1 double crochet into next 4 stitches, work 2 double crochets together, repeat from * to end. 30 stitches.

Rounds 28 – 29: As round 9.

Round 30: * Work 1 double crochet into next 3 stitches, work 2 double crochets together, repeat from * to end. 24 stitches.

Rounds 31 – 32: As round 9.

Round 33: * Work 1 double crochet into next 2 stitches, work 2 double crochets together, repeat from * to end. 18 stitches.

Rounds 34 – 41: As round 9.

Fasten off leaving a long length of yarn.

ARMS – (MAKE 2)

Using 4mm (US G/6) hook and yarn B make a magic ring.

Round 1: Work 4 double crochets into the ring. 4 stitches.

Round 2: * Work 2 double crochets into next stitch, repeat from * to end. 8 stitches.

Round 3: Work 1 double crochet into each stitch.

Round 4: As round 3.

Change to yarn A.

Rounds 5 – 23: As round 3.

Fasten off leaving a long length of yarn.

LEGS – (MAKE 2)

Using 4mm (US G/6) hook and yarn B make a magic ring.

Round 1: Work 6 double crochets into the ring. 6 stitches.

Round 2: * Work 2 double crochets into next stitch, repeat from * to end. 12 stitches.

Round 3: * Work 1 double crochet into next stitch, work 2 double crochets into next stitch, repeat from * to end. 18 stitches.

Round 4: Work 1 double crochet into each stitch.

Rounds 5 – 6: As round 4.

Round 7: Work 1 double crochet into next 5 stitches, (work 2 double crochets together) 4 times, work 1 double crochet into next 5 stitches. 14 stitches.

Round 8: Work 1 double crochet into next 5 stitches, (work 2 double crochets together) twice, work 1 double crochet into next 5 stitches. 12 stitches.

Round 9: As round 4.

Change to yarn A.

Rounds 10 – 19: As round 4.

Fasten off leaving a long length of yarn.

SPOTS – (MAKE 10)

Using 4mm (US G/6) hook and yarn B make a magic ring.

Round 1: Work 6 double crochets into the ring. 6 stitches.

Round 2: * Work 2 double crochets into next stitch, repeat from * to end. 12 stitches. Fasten off leaving a long length of yarn.

SCARF

Using 4mm (US G/6) hook and yarn D make 61 chains.

Row 1: Work 1 double crochet into second chain from hook, work 1 double crochet into each stitch, turn. 60 stitches.

Row 2: Make 1 chain, work 1 double crochet into each stitch, turn.

Fasten off leaving a long length of yarn.

TAIL

Using yarn A cut 6 lengths of yarn each 30cm/12in long.

Fold yarn in half, attach to back of body, pulling through using a crochet hook. Knot in place, then plait to end, securing with a knot. Cut the strands to neaten.

MAKING UP

Sew mouth to head 1 row below eyes. Stuff body, sew head to body. Sew 8 spots to body, bring all loose yarn to neck, tie together and trim. Sew 2 spots to head, bring loose yarn to bottom of head, tie together and trim. Sew horns to top of head. Pinch ears to create a fold, sew ears to side of head. Stuff first 4 rounds of arms, sew arms to body. Stuff legs, sew legs in sitting position to lower part of body. Tie scarf around neck and sew in place if desired.

ELEPHANT

This nosy elephant has big floppy ears and a long trunk that can be increased or decreased in size to your liking. Add some character to your elephant by making a personalized hair bow or bow tie.

SKILL LEVEL: SOME EXPERIENCE

YOU'LL NEED:

YARN

Rowan Handknit Cotton or any No.3
light weight yarn
A – 2 × 50g of Feather 373
B – 1 × 50g of Ecru 251
C – 1 × 50g of Ballet Pink 372
D – 1 × 50g of Sugar 303

HOOK

4mm (US G/6) hook

EXTRAS

Toy stuffing
2 × Black safety eyes
Stitch marker

ELEPHANT

SIZE
23cm/8¾in high

TENSION
18 sts and 20 rows to 10cm/4in
Measured over double crochet using 4mm (US G/6) hook.

HEAD
Using 4mm (US G/6) hook and yarn A make a magic ring.

Round 1: Work 6 double crochets into the ring. 6 stitches.

Round 2: * Work 2 double crochets into next stitch, repeat from * to end. 12 stitches.

Round 3: * Work 1 double crochet into next stitch, work 2 double crochets into next stitch, repeat from * to end. 18 stitches.

Round 4: * Work 1 double crochet into next 2 stitches, work 2 double crochets into next stitch, repeat from * to end. 24 stitches.

Round 5: * Work 1 double crochet into next 3 stitches, work 2 double crochets into next stitch, repeat from * to end. 30 stitches.

Round 6: * Work 1 double crochet into next 4 stitches, work 2 double crochets into next stitch, repeat from * to end. 36 stitches.

Round 7: * Work 1 double crochet into next 5 stitches, work 2 double crochets into next stitch, repeat from * to end. 42 stitches.

Round 8: Work 1 double crochet into each stitch.

Rounds 9 – 19: As round 8.

Attach safety eyes between rounds 13 and 14 with 7 stitches between them.

Round 20: * Work 1 double crochet into next 5 stitches, work 2 double crochets together, repeat from * to end. 36 stitches.

Round 21: * Work 1 double crochet into next 4 stitches, work 2 double crochets together, repeat from * to end. 30 stitches.

Round 22: * Work 1 double crochet into next 3 stitches, work 2 double crochets together, repeat from * to end. 24 stitches.

Start to stuff and continue stuffing as you work.

Round 23: * Work 1 double crochet into next 2 stitches, work 2 double crochets together, repeat from * to end. 18 stitches.

Round 24: * Work 1 double crochet into next stitch, work 2 double crochets together, repeat from * to end. 12 stitches.

Round 25: * Work 2 double crochets together, repeat from * to end. 6 stitches.

Fasten off leaving a long length of yarn. Sew a running stitch around last round, pull tight to secure and close hole.

TRUNK

Using 4mm (US G/6) hook and yarn A make a magic ring.

Round 1: Work 4 double crochets into the ring. 4 stitches.

Round 2: * Work 2 double crochets into next stitch, repeat from * to end. 8 stitches.

Round 3: Work 1 double crochet into each stitch.

Rounds 4 – 14: As round 3.

Round 15: * Work 1 double crochet into next stitch, work 2 double crochets into next stitch, repeat from * to end. 18 stitches.

Round 16: Work 2 double crochets into next stitch, work 1 double crochet into next 10 stitches, work 2 double crochets into next stitch. 14 stitches.

Fasten off leaving a long length of yarn.

OUTER EAR – (MAKE 2)

Using 4mm (US G/6) hook and yarn A make a magic ring.

Round 1: Work 6 double crochets into the ring. 6 stitches.

Round 2: * Work 2 double crochets into next stitch, repeat from * to end. 12 stitches.

Round 3: * Work 1 double crochet into next stitch, work 2 double crochets into next stitch, repeat from * to end. 18 stitches.

Round 4: * Work 1 double crochet into next 2 stitches, work 2 double crochets into next stitch, repeat from * to end. 24 stitches.

Round 5: * Work 1 double crochet into next 3 stitches, work 2 double crochets into next stitch, repeat from * to end. 30 stitches.

Round 6: * Work 1 double crochet into next 4 stitches, work 2 double crochets into next stitch, repeat from * to end. 36 stitches.

Round 7: * Work 1 double crochet into next 5 stitches, work 2 double crochets into next stitch, repeat from * to end. 42 stitches.

Round 8: * Work 1 double crochet into next 6 stitches, work 2 double crochets into next stitch, repeat from * to end. 48 stitches.

Round 9: Work 1 double crochet into each stitch.

Round 10: As round 9.

Fasten off leaving a long length of yarn.

INNER EAR – (MAKE 2)

Using 4mm (US G/6) hook and yarn C make a magic ring.

Round 1: Work 6 double crochets into the ring. 6 stitches.

Round 2: * Work 2 double crochets into next stitch, repeat from * to end. 12 stitches.

Round 3: * Work 1 double crochet into next stitch, work 2 double crochets into next stitch, repeat from * to end. 18 stitches.

Round 4: * Work 1 double crochet into next 2 stitches, work 2 double crochets into next stitch, repeat from * to end. 24 stitches.

Round 5: * Work 1 double crochet into next 3 stitches, work 2 double crochets into next stitch, repeat from * to end. 30 stitches.

Round 6: * Work 1 double crochet into next 4 stitches, work 2 double crochets into next stitch, repeat from * to end. 36 stitches.

Round 7: * Work 1 double crochet into next 5 stitches, work 2 double crochets into next stitch, repeat from * to end. 42 stitches.

Round 8: * Work 1 double crochet into next 6 stitches, work 2 double crochets into next stitch, repeat from * to end. 48 stitches.
Fasten off leaving a long length of yarn.

BODY

Using 4mm (US G/6) hook and yarn A make a magic ring.

Round 1: Work 6 double crochets into the ring. 6 stitches.

Round 2: * Work 2 double crochets into next stitch, repeat from * to end. 12 stitches.

Round 3: * Work 1 double crochet into next stitch, work 2 double crochets into next stitch, repeat from * to end. 18 stitches.

Round 4: * Work 1 double crochet into next 2 stitches, work 2 double crochets into next stitch, repeat from * to end. 24 stitches.

Round 5: * Work 1 double crochet into next 3 stitches, work 2 double crochets into next stitch, repeat from * to end. 30 stitches.

Round 6: * Work 1 double crochet into next 4 stitches, work 2 double crochets into next stitch, repeat from * to end. 36 stitches.

Round 7: * Work 1 double crochet into next 5 stitches, work 2 double crochets into next stitch, repeat from * to end. 42 stitches.

Round 8: * Work 1 double crochet into next 6 stitches, work 2 double crochets into next stitch, repeat from * to end. 48 stitches.

Round 9: Work 1 double crochet into each stitch.

Rounds 10 – 20: As round 9.

Round 21: * Work 1 double crochet into next 6 stitches, work 2 double crochets together, repeat from * to end. 42 stitches.

Rounds 22 – 23: As round 9.

Round 24: * Work 1 double crochet into next 5 stitches, work 2 double crochets together, repeat from * to end. 36 stitches.

Rounds 25 – 26: As round 9.

Round 27: * Work 1 double crochet into next 4 stitches, work 2 double crochets together, repeat from * to end. 30 stitches.

Rounds 28 – 29: As round 9.

Round 30: * Work 1 double crochet into next 3 stitches, work 2 double crochets together, repeat from * to end. 24 stitches.

Rounds 31 – 32: As round 9.

Round 33: * Work 1 double crochet into next 2 stitches, work 2 double crochets together, repeat from * to end. 18 stitches.

Rounds 34 – 35: As round 9.
Fasten off leaving a long length of yarn.

ARMS – (MAKE 2)

Using 4mm (US G/6) hook and yarn B make a magic ring.

Round 1: Work 6 double crochets into the ring. 6 stitches.

Round 2: * Work 2 double crochets into next stitch, repeat from * to end. 12 stitches.

Round 3: Working into back loop only, work 1 double crochet into each stitch.

Round 4: Work 1 double crochet into each stitch.
Change to yarn A.

Rounds 5 – 15: As round 4.
Fasten off leaving a long length of yarn.

LEGS – (MAKE 2)

Using 4mm (US G/6) hook and yarn B make a magic ring.

Round 1: Work 6 double crochets into the ring. 6 stitches.

Round 2: * Work 2 double crochets into next stitch, repeat from * to end. 12 stitches.

Round 3: * Work 1 double crochet into next stitch, work 2 double crochets into next stitch, repeat from * to end. 18 stitches.

Round 4: Working into back loop only, work 1 double crochet into each stitch.

Round 5: Work 1 double crochet into each stitch.

Change to yarn A.

Rounds 6 – 15: As round 4.

Fasten off leaving a long length of yarn.

BOW

Using 4mm (US G/6) hook and yarn D make 25 chains.

Row 1: Work 1 double crochet into second chain from hook, work 1 double crochet into each stitch, turn. 24 stitches.

Row 2: Make 1 chain, work 1 double crochet into each stitch, turn.

Rows 3 – 5: As row 2.

Row 6: Make 1 chain, work 1 double crochet into each stitch, **do not turn**.

Fold in half and slip stitch last row to starting chain.

Fasten off leaving a long length of yarn. Turn bow section so that stitches lie on the back of the bow.

STRAP

Using 4mm (US G/6) hook and yarn D make 9 chains.

Row 1: Work 1 double crochet into second chain from hook, work 1 double crochet into each stitch, turn. 8 stitches.

Row 2: Make 1 chain, work 1 double crochet into each stitch, turn.

Wrap strap around bow and slip stitch edges together around bow.

Fasten off leaving a long length of yarn.

TAIL

Using yarn A cut 6 lengths of yarn each 30cm/12in long.

Fold yarn in half, attach to back of body, pulling through using a crochet hook. Knot in place, then plait to end, securing with a knot. Cut the strands to neaten.

MAKING UP

Attach trunk to head below eyes, ensuring increased stitches from last round are facing downwards, bend trunk downwards. Sew inner ears to outer ears, pinch ears to create a fold, sew ears to side of head. Stuff body, sew head to body. Stuff first 4 rounds of arms, sew arms to body. Stuff legs, sew legs in sitting position to lower part of body. Sew bow to head.

UNICORN

Colourful and bright, this unicorn has it all. Personalize your unicorn to your taste and make sure to give the horn a magic touch of colour! Its multicoloured plaited tail and long, curly mane give the unicorn funky finishing touches.

SKILL LEVEL: SOME EXPERIENCE

YOU'LL NEED:

YARN

Rowan Cotton Glace or any No.3
light weight yarn
A – 1 x 50g of Rose 861
B – 1 x 50g of Poppy 741
C – 1 x 50g of Mineral 856
D – 1 x 50g of Persimmon 832
E – 1 x 50g of Shoot 814
F – 1 x 50g of Aqua 858
G – 2 x 50g of Bleached 726
H – 1 x 50g of Black 727

HOOK

3.5mm (US E/4) hook

EXTRAS

Toy stuffing
2 x Black safety eyes
Stitch marker

UNICORN

SIZE
23cm/9in from head to feet when standing

TENSION
24 sts and 26 rows to 10cm/4in
Measured over double crochet using 3.5mm
(US E/4) hook.

HEAD
Using 3.5mm (US E/4) hook and yarn C
make a magic ring.
Round 1: Work 6 double crochets into the
ring. 6 stitches.
Round 2: * Work 2 double crochets into
next stitch, repeat from * to end. 12 stitches.
Round 3: * Work 1 double crochet into next
stitch, work 2 double crochets into next
stitch, repeat from * to end. 18 stitches.
Round 4: * Work 1 double crochet into next
2 stitches, work 2 double crochets into next
stitch, repeat from * to end. 24 stitches.
Round 5: * Work 1 double crochet into next

3 stitches, work 2 double crochets into next
stitch, repeat from * to end. 30 stitches.
Round 6: Work 1 double crochet into
each stitch.
Rounds 7 – 9: As round 6.
Change to yarn G.
Round 10: * Work 1 double crochet into
next stitch, work 2 double crochets into next
stitch, repeat from * to end. 45 stitches.
Rounds 11 – 22: As round 6.
Attach safety eyes between rounds 11 and
12 with 12 stitches between them.
Round 23: * Work 1 double crochet into
next stitch, work 2 double crochets together,
repeat from * to end. 30 stitches.
Round 24: * Work 1 double crochet into
next 3 stitches, work 2 double crochets
together, repeat from * to end. 24 stitches.

Start to stuff and continue stuffing as
you work.

Round 25: * Work 1 double crochet into next 2 stitches, work 2 double crochets together, repeat from * to end. 18 stitches.

Round 26: * Work 1 double crochet into next stitch, work 2 double crochets together, repeat from * to end. 12 stitches.

Round 27: * Work 2 double crochets together, repeat from * to end. 6 stitches. Sew a running stitch around last round, pull tight to secure and close hole.

HORN

Using 3.5mm (US E/4) hook and yarn A make a magic ring.

Round 1: Work 4 double crochets into the ring. 4 stitches.

Round 2: Work 1 double crochet into each stitch.

Round 3: * Work 1 double crochet into next stitch, work 2 double crochets into next stitch, repeat from * to end. 6 stitches.

Round 4: As round 2.

Round 5: * Work 1 double crochet into next 2 stitches, work 2 double crochets into next stitch, repeat from * to end. 8 stitches.

Round 6: As round 2.

Round 7: * Work 1 double crochet into next 3 stitches, work 2 double crochets into next stitch, repeat from * to end. 10 stitches.

Round 8: As round 2.

Round 9: * Work 1 double crochet into next 4 stitches, work 2 double crochets into next stitch, repeat from * to end. 10 stitches.

Round 10: As round 2.
Fasten off leaving a long length of yarn.

EARS – (MAKE 2)

Using 3.5mm (US E/4) hook and yarn G make a magic ring.

Round 1: Work 4 double crochets into the ring. 4 stitches.

Round 2: Work 1 double crochet into each stitch.

Round 3: * Work 1 double crochet into next stitch, work 2 double crochets into next stitch, repeat from * to end. 6 stitches.

Round 4: * Work 1 double crochet into next 2 stitches, work 2 double crochets into next stitch, repeat from * to end. 8 stitches.

Round 5: * Work 1 double crochet into next 3 stitches, work 2 double crochets into next stitch, repeat from * to end. 10 stitches.

Rounds 6 – 9: As round 2.
Fasten off leaving a long length of yarn.

BODY

Using 3.5mm (US E/4) hook and yarn G make a magic ring.

Round 1: Work 6 double crochets into the ring. 6 stitches.

Round 2: * Work 2 double crochets into next stitch, repeat from * to end. 12 stitches.

Round 3: * Work 1 double crochet into next stitch, work 2 double crochets into next stitch, repeat from * to end. 18 stitches.

Round 4: * Work 1 double crochet into next 2 stitches, work 2 double crochets into next stitch, repeat from * to end. 24 stitches.

Round 5: * Work 1 double crochet into next 3 stitches, work 2 double crochets into next stitch, repeat from * to end. 30 stitches.

Round 6: * Work 1 double crochet into next 4 stitches, work 2 double crochets into next stitch, repeat from * to end. 36 stitches.

Round 7: * Work 1 double crochet into next 5 stitches, work 2 double crochets into next stitch, repeat from * to end. 42 stitches.

Round 8: * Work 1 double crochet into next 6 stitches, work 2 double crochets into next stitch, repeat from * to end. 48 stitches.

Round 9: * Work 1 double crochet into next 7 stitches, work 2 double crochets into next stitch, repeat from * to end. 54 stitches.

Round 10: Work 1 double crochet into each stitch.

Rounds 11 – 21: As round 10.

Round 22: * Work 1 double crochet into next 7 stitches, work 2 double crochets together, repeat from * to end. 48 stitches.
Rounds 23 – 24: As round 10.
Round 25: * Work 1 double crochet into next 6 stitches, work 2 double crochets together, repeat from * to end. 42 stitches.
Rounds 26 – 27: As round 10.
Round 28: * Work 1 double crochet into next 5 stitches, work 2 double crochets together, repeat from * to end. 36 stitches.
Rounds 29 – 30: As round 10.
Round 31: * Work 1 double crochet into next 4 stitches, work 2 double crochets together, repeat from * to end. 30 stitches.
Rounds 32 – 33: As round 10.
Round 34: * Work 1 double crochet into next 3 stitches, work 2 double crochets together, repeat from * to end. 24 stitches.
Rounds 35 – 36: As round 10.
Fasten off leaving a long length of yarn.

ARMS – (MAKE 1 USING YARN F AND 1 USING YARN D)

Using 3.5mm (US E/4) hook and yarn indicated make a magic ring.
Round 1: Work 6 double crochets into the ring. 6 stitches.
Round 2: * Work 2 double crochets into next stitch, repeat from * to end. 12 stitches.
Round 3: Work 1 double crochet into each stitch.
Rounds 4 – 5: As round 3.
Change to yarn G.
Rounds 6 – 21: As round 3.
Fasten off leaving a long length of yarn.

LEGS – (MAKE 1 USING YARN E AND 1 USING YARN B)

Using 3.5mm (US E/4) hook and yarn indicated make a magic ring.
Round 1: Work 6 double crochets into the ring. 6 stitches.
Round 2: * Work 2 double crochets into next stitch, repeat from * to end. 12 stitches.
Round 3: * Work 1 double crochet into next stitch, work 2 double crochets into next stitch, repeat from * to end. 18 stitches.
Round 4: Work 1 double crochet into each stitch.
Rounds 5 – 6: As round 4.
Change to yarn G.
Rounds 7 – 26: As round 4.
Fasten off leaving a long length of yarn.

MANE – (MAKE 1 IN EACH OF YARNS A, B, C, D, E AND F)

Using 3.5mm (US E/4) hook and yarn A make 41 chains.
Row 1: Work 2 double crochets into second chain from hook, * work 2 double crochets into next stitch, repeat from * to end. 80 stitches.
Fasten off leaving a long length of yarn.

TAIL

Cut 1 length in each of yarns A, B, C, D, E and F each 30cm/12in long.
Fold yarn in half, attach to back of body, pulling through using a crochet hook. Knot in place, then plait to end, securing with a knot. Cut the strands to neaten.

MAKING UP

Using yarn H, embroider 2 X shapes to face to create nostrils. Attach horn to top of head. Stuff body, sew head to body. Pinch base of ears, sew ears to side of head. Stuff first 5 rounds of arms only, sew arms to body. Stuff legs, sew legs to lower part of body. Sew mane to neck.

SENSORY TOY

A quick and easy make, using materials you have at home. Two crochet squares are joined, with ribbon and fabric tags placed around the edges. Using fabrics with different textures is a great idea and will create a unique sensory toy.

SKILL LEVEL: EASY

YOU'LL NEED:

YARN
1 x 50g of Rowan Handknit Cotton or any
No.4 medium weight yarn
(photographed in Rosso 215)

HOOK
4.5mm (US 7) hook

EXTRAS
Ribbons and fabric strips of your choice
for tags
Matching sewing thread for the base

SENSORY TOY

SIZE
12cm/4¾in wide and 12cm/4¾in high

TENSION
16 sts and 21 rows to 10cm/4in
Measured over double crochet using 4.5mm (US 7) hook.

BASE – (MAKE 2)
Using 4.5mm (US 7) hook make 21 chains.
Row 1: Work 1 double crochet into second hook from chain, work 1 double crochet into each stitch to end. 20 stitches.
Row 2: Make 1 chain, work 1 double crochet into each stitch to end.
Rep last row until work measures 12cm/4¾in. Fasten off.

MAKING UP
Press as described on page 17.
Attach strips of ribbon and fabric folded in half, secure using pins to the edges on one side of the base, using matching sewing thread, secure into place. Place the second base on top of the first, join using mattress stitch going around the ribbon/fabric. When you get to this point, you can secure the other side of the base using sewing thread if needed.

BEAN BAGS

Bean bags are a simple childhood favourite for most children. They can be used for a number of different games, for all ages. Fill your bean bags with toy stuffing or dried lentils in a sealed bag.

SKILL LEVEL: SOME EXPERIENCE

YOU'LL NEED:

YARN
Rowan Summerlite DK or any No.3
light weight yarn
A – I x 50g Favourite Denims 469
B – I x 50g Silvery Blue 468

HOOK
3mm (US C/2) hook

EXTRAS
Toy stuffing

BEAN BAGS

SIZE
10cm/4in high and 10cm/4in wide

TENSION
22sts and 24 rows to 10cm/4in
Measured over double crochet using 3mm (US C/2) hook and yarn held double throughout.

SIDES – (MAKE 4)
Using 3mm (US C/2) hook and yarn A held double make 2 chains.

Row 1: Make 1 chain, work 2 double crochets into next stitch. 2 stitches.

Row 2: Make 1 chain, work 1 double crochet into next 2 stitches.

Row 3: Make 1 chain, work 2 double crochets into next 2 stitches. 4 stitches.

Row 4: Make 1 chain, work 1 double crochet into next 4 stitches.

Row 5: Make 1 chain, work 2 double crochets into next stitch, work 1 double crochet into next 2 stitches, work 2 double crochets into last stitch. 6 stitches.

Row 6: Make 1 chain, work 1 double crochet into next 6 stitches.

Row 7: Make 1 chain, work 2 double crochets into next stitch, work 1 double crochet into next 4 stitches, work 2 double crochets into last stitch. 8 stitches.

Row 8: Make 1 chain, work 1 double crochet into next 8 stitches.

Row 9: Make 1 chain, work 2 double crochets into next stitch, work 1 double crochet into next 6 stitches, work 2 double crochets into last stitch. 10 stitches.

Row 10: Make 1 chain, work 1 double crochet into next 10 stitches.

Row 11: Make 1 chain, work 2 double crochets into next stitch, work 1 double crochet into next 8 stitches, work 2 double crochets into last stitch. 12 stitches.

Row 12: Make 1 chain, work 1 double crochet into next 12 stitches.

Row 13: Make 1 chain, work 2 double crochets into next stitch, work 1 double crochet into next 10 stitches, work 2 double crochets into last stitch. 14 stitches.

Row 14: Make 1 chain, work 1 double crochet into next 14 stitches.

Row 15: Make 1 chain, work 2 double crochets into next stitch, work 1 double crochet into next 12 stitches, work 2 double crochets into last stitch. 16 stitches.

Row 16: Make 1 chain, work 1 double crochet into next 16 stitches.

Row 17: Make 1 chain, work 2 double crochets into next stitch, work 1 double crochet into next 14 stitches, work 2 double crochets into last stitch. 18 stitches.

Row 18: Make 1 chain, work 1 double crochet into next 18 stitches.

Row 19: Make 1 chain, work 2 double crochets into next stitch, work 1 double crochet into next 16 stitches, work 2 double crochets into last stitch. 20 stitches.

Row 20: Make 1 chain, work 1 double crochet into next 20 stitches.

Row 21: Make 1 chain, work 2 double crochets into next stitch, work 1 double crochet into next 18 stitches, work 2 double crochets into last stitch. 22 stitches.

Row 22: Make 1 chain, work 1 double crochet into next 22 stitches.

Row 23: Make 1 chain, work 2 double crochets into next stitch, work 1 double crochet into next 20 stitches, work 2 double crochets into last stitch. 24 stitches.

Row 24: Make 1 chain, work 1 double crochet into next 24 stitches.
Fasten off.

MAKING UP

Press as described on page 17.
Holding sides together with wrong sides facing, join in yarn B held double and work 24 double crochets through both panels to join.
Repeat this step with a second panel then join all 3 together to form a pyramid.
Hold the fourth panel as the base and join 2 sides in the same way, start stuffing your bean bag as you join the last seam.
Fasten off.

STACKING RINGS

A great concentration game for young children. These stacking rings can be given a personal touch and made in whichever colours you like. Be sure to stuff them well, so that they keep their shape.

SKILL LEVEL: SOME EXPERIENCE

YOU'LL NEED:

YARN

Stylecraft Special DK or any No.3
light weight yarn
A – 1 × 100g of Sherbet 1034
B – 1 × 100g of Lemon 1020
C – 1 × 100g of Apricot 1026
D – 1 × 100g of Clematis 1390
E – 1 × 100g of Wisteria 1432

HOOK

4mm (US G/6) hook

EXTRAS

Toy stuffing

STACKING RINGS

SIZE

Cone – 18cm/7in high
Rings – largest (ring 1) – 12cm/4¾in diameter, smallest (ring 5) – 9cm/3½in diameter

TENSION

18 sts and 20 rows to 10cm/4in
Measured over double crochet using 4mm (US G/6) hook.

CONE

Base

Using 4mm (US G/6) hook and yarn A make a magic loop, work 6 double crochets into the loop. 6 stitches.

Round 1: Work 2 double crochets into each stitch. 12 stitches.

Round 2: * Work 2 double crochets into next stitch, work 1 double crochet into next stitch, repeat from * to end. 18 stitches.

Round 3: * Work 1 double crochet into next 2 stitches, work 2 double crochets into next stitch, repeat from * to end. 24 stitches.

Round 4: * Work 2 double crochets into next stitch, work 1 double crochet into next 3 stitches, repeat from * to end. 30 stitches.

Round 5: * Work 1 double crochet into next 4 stitches, work 2 double crochets into next stitch, repeat from * to end. 36 stitches.

Round 6: * Work 2 double crochets into next stitch, work 1 double crochet into next 5 stitches, repeat from * to end. 42 stitches.

Round 7: * Work 1 double crochet into next 6 stitches, work 2 double crochets into next stitch, repeat from * to end. 48 stitches. Fasten off.

Body

Using 4mm (US G/6) hook and yarn A make a magic loop, work 6 double crochets into the loop. 6 stitches.

Round 1: Work 2 double crochets into each stitch. 12 stitches.

Round 2: * Work 2 double crochets into

next stitch, work 1 double crochet into next stitch, repeat from * to end. 18 stitches.

Round 3: Work 1 double crochet into each stitch.

Rounds 4 – 6: As round 3.

Round 7: * Work 1 double crochet into next 2 stitches, work 2 double crochets into next stitch, repeat from * to end. 24 stitches.

Rounds 8 – 11: As round 3.

Round 12: * Work 2 double crochets into next stitch, work 1 double crochet into next 3 stitches, repeat from * to end. 30 stitches.

Rounds 13 – 18: As round 3.

Round 19: * Work 1 double crochet into next 4 stitches, work 2 double crochets into next stitch, repeat from * to end. 36 stitches.

Rounds 20 – 25: As round 3.

Round 26: * Work 2 double crochets into next stitch, work 1 double crochet into next 5 stitches, repeat from * to end. 42 stitches.

Rounds 27 – 32: As round 3.

Round 33: * Work 1 double crochet into next 6 stitches, work 2 double crochets into next stitch, repeat from * to end. 48 stitches.

Round 34: As round 3.

Round 35: As round 3, **do not fasten off**. Stuff firmly.

Round 36: Working into back loops only, work a round of double crochets around both base and body to join.

Fasten off leaving a long length of yarn.

RING 1

Using 4mm (US G/6) hook and yarn A make 48 chains, join with a slip stitch to first chain.

Round 1: Make 1 chain, work 1 double crochet into each chain, join with a slip stitch. 48 stitches.

Round 2: Make 1 chain, * work 2 double crochets into first stitch, work 1 double crochet into next stitch, repeat from * to end, join with a slip stitch. 72 stitches.

Round 3: Make 1 chain, work 1 double

crochet into each stitch, join with a slip stitch.

Rounds 4 – 12: As round 3.

Round 13: Make 1 chain, * work 1 double crochet into next stitch, work 2 double crochets together, repeat from * to end, join with a slip stitch. 48 stitches.

Round 14: As round 3.

Fasten off leaving a long length of yarn.

RING 2

Using 4mm (US G/6) hook and yarn B make 44 chains, join with a slip stitch to first chain.

Round 1: Make 1 chain, work 1 double crochet into each chain, join with a slip stitch. 44 stitches.

Round 2: Make 1 chain, * work 2 double crochets into first stitch, work 1 double crochet into next stitch, repeat from * to end, join with a slip stitch. 66 stitches.

Round 3: Make 1 chain, work 1 double crochet into each stitch, join with a slip stitch.

Rounds 4 – 12: As round 3.

Round 13: Make 1 chain, * work 1 double crochet into next stitch, work 2 double crochets together, repeat from * to end, join with a slip stitch. 44 stitches.

Round 14: As round 3.

Fasten off leaving a long length of yarn.

RING 3

Using 4mm (US G/6) hook and yarn C make 42 chains, join with a slip stitch to first chain.

Round 1: Make 1 chain, work 1 double crochet into each chain, join with a slip stitch. 42 stitches.

Round 2: Make 1 chain, * work 2 double crochets into first stitch, work 1 double crochet into next stitch, repeat from * to end, join with a slip stitch. 63 stitches.

Round 3: Make 1 chain, work 1 double crochet into each stitch, join with a slip stitch.

Rounds 4 – 12: As round 3.

Round 13: Make 1 chain, * work 1 double

crochet into next stitch, work 2 double crochets together, repeat from * to end, join with a slip stitch. 42 stitches.

Round 14: As round 3.

Fasten off leaving a long length of yarn.

RING 4

Using 4mm (US G/6) hook and yarn D make 38 chains, join with a slip stitch to first chain.

Round 1: Make 1 chain, work 1 double crochet into each chain, join with a slip stitch. 38 stitches.

Round 2: Make 1 chain, * work 2 double crochets into first stitch, work 1 double crochet into next stitch, repeat from * to end, join with a slip stitch. 57 stitches.

Round 3: Make 1 chain, work 1 double crochet into each stitch, join with a slip stitch.

Rounds 4 – 12: As round 3.

Round 13: Make 1 chain, * work 1 double crochet into next stitch, work 2 double crochets together, repeat from * to end, join with a slip stitch. 38 stitches.

Round 14: As round 3.

Fasten off leaving a long length of yarn.

RING 5

Using 4mm (US G/6) hook and yarn E make 32 chains, join with a slip stitch to first chain.

Round 1: Make 1 chain, work 1 double crochet into each chain, join with a slip stitch. 38 stitches.

Round 2: Make 1 chain, * work 2 double crochets into first stitch, work 1 double crochet into next stitch, repeat from * to end, join with a slip stitch. 48 stitches.

Round 3: Make 1 chain, work 1 double crochet into each stitch, join with a slip stitch.

Rounds 4 – 12: As round 3.

Round 13: Make 1 chain, * work 1 double

crochet into next stitch, work 2 double crochets together, repeat from * to end, join with a slip stitch. 32 stitches.

Round 14: As round 3.

Fasten off leaving a long length of yarn.

MAKING UP

For each ring, ensuring wrong side of work is on the inside, sew first and last rounds together using whip stitch, stuffing as you go. Sew ring 1 to base of cone.

Sew in loose ends.

STACKING CUBES

Cubes to stack and knock down again and again! Made from Rowan's Summerlite DK, worked in squares and joined with double crochet, these cubes can be a great way to use up leftover yarn.

SKILL LEVEL: EASY

YOU'LL NEED:

YARN
Rowan Summerlite DK or any No.3
light weight yarn
A – 1 x 50g of Plaster 452
B – 1 x 50g of Seashell 466
C – 1 x 50g of Linen 460
D – 1 x 50g of White 465

You should be able to make 3 cubes with this quantity of yarn.

HOOK
3.5mm (US E/4) hook

EXTRAS
Toy stuffing

STACKING CUBES

SIZE
10cm/4in x 10cm/4in

TENSION
22 sts and 25 rows to 10cm/4in
Measured over double crochet using 3.5mm (US E/4) hook

SQUARES – (MAKE 2 EACH IN A, B AND C)
Using 3.5mm (US E/4) hook, make 23 stitches.
Row 1: Work 1 double crochet into second chain from hook, work 1 double crochet into each stitch to end. 22 stitches.
Row 2: Make 1 chain, work 1 double crochet into each stitch to end.
Rep last row 23 times more.
Each square should measure 10cm x 10cm/ 4in x 4in.

MAKING UP
Press as described on page 17.

Using yarn D and 3.5mm (US E/4) hook, work squares together as described below. Holding wrong sides together, work 25 double crochets along seam, repeat for each seam.

Attach block As to the tops of block Cs. Attach the 2 block Bs to either side of one of the block As. Attach the bottom of these block Bs to the sides of this block C. Attach the top of this block A to the bottom of other block C.
Fold cube together and join all sides, stuffing as you go.

COLOUR GAME

Worked in a bright medium weight cotton, these baskets and balls are a great way to teach young children about colour recognition. They will have lots of fun simply throwing the coloured balls into the matching coloured baskets.

SKILL LEVEL: SOME EXPERIENCE

YOU'LL NEED:

YARN
3 x 50g of Rowan Cotton Glace or any
No.3 light weight yarn
(photographed in Persimmon 832, Mineral
856 and Shoot 814)

*I made only 3 balls in each colour, but estimate
you can make a further 2.*

HOOK
3mm (US C/2) hook

EXTRAS
Toy stuffing

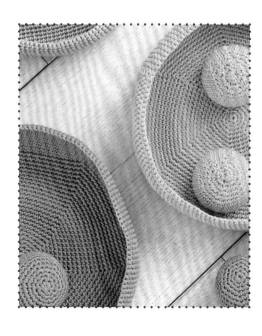

COLOUR GAME

SIZE

Basket – 22cm/8¾in circumference and 5cm/2in high

Balls – 15cm/6in in diameter

TENSION

25 sts and 25 rows to 10cm/4in
Measured over double crochet using 3mm (US C/2) hook.

BASKET

Using 3mm (US C/2) hook and yarn of choice make 3 chains, join with a slip stitch into first chain made to form a ring.

Round 1: Make 1 chain, work 6 double crochets into the ring. 6 stitches.

Round 2: Make 1 chain, work 2 double crochets into each stitch to end, join with a slip stitch. 12 stitches.

Round 3: Make 1 chain, * work 1 double crochet into next stitch, work 2 double crochets into following stitch, repeat from * to end, join with a slip stitch. 18 stitches.

Round 4: Make 1 chain, * work 1 double crochet into next 2 stitches, work 2 double crochets into following stitch, repeat from * to end, join with a slip stitch. 24 stitches.

Round 5: Make 1 chain, * work 1 double crochet into next 3 stitches, work 2 double crochets into following stitch, repeat from * to end, join with a slip stitch. 30 stitches.

Round 6: Make 1 chain, * work 1 double crochet into next 4 stitches, work 2 double crochets into following stitch, repeat from * to end, join with a slip stitch. 36 stitches.

Round 7: Make 1 chain, * work 1 double crochet into next 5 stitches, work 2 double crochets into following stitch, repeat from * to end, join with a slip stitch. 42 stitches.

Round 8: Make 1 chain, * work 1 double crochet into next 6 stitches, work 2 double crochets into following stitch, repeat from * to end, join with a slip stitch. 48 stitches.

Round 9: Make 1 chain, * work 1 double

crochet into next 7 stitches, work 2 double crochets into following stitch, repeat from * to end, join with a slip stitch. 54 stitches.

Round 10: Make 1 chain, * work 1 double crochet into next 8 stitches, work 2 double crochets into following stitch, repeat from * to end, join with a slip stitch. 60 stitches.

Round 11: Make 1 chain, * work 1 double crochet into next 9 stitches, work 2 double crochets into following stitch, repeat from * to end, join with a slip stitch. 66 stitches.

Round 12: Make 1 chain, * work 1 double crochet into next 10 stitches, work 2 double crochets into following stitch, repeat from * to end, join with a slip stitch. 72 stitches.

Round 13: Make 1 chain, * work 1 double crochet into next 11 stitches, work 2 double crochets into following stitch, repeat from * to end, join with a slip stitch. 78 stitches.

Round 14: Make 1 chain, * work 1 double crochet into next 12 stitches, work 2 double crochets into following stitch, repeat from * to end, join with a slip stitch. 84 stitches.

Round 15: Make 1 chain, * work 1 double crochet into next 13 stitches, work 2 double crochets into following stitch, repeat from * to end, join with a slip stitch. 90 stitches.

Round 16: Make 1 chain, * work 1 double crochet into next 14 stitches, work 2 double crochets into following stitch, repeat from * to end, join with a slip stitch. 96 stitches.

Round 17: Make 1 chain, * work 1 double crochet into next 15 stitches, work 2 double crochets into following stitch, repeat from * to end, join with a slip stitch. 102 stitches.

Round 18: Make 1 chain, * work 1 double crochet into next 16 stitches, work 2 double crochets into following stitch, repeat from * to end, join with a slip stitch. 108 stitches.

Round 19: Make 1 chain, * work 1 double crochet into next 17 stitches, work 2 double

crochets into following stitch, repeat from * to end, join with a slip stitch. 114 stitches.

Round 20: Make 1 chain, * work 1 double crochet into next 18 stitches, work 2 double crochets into following stitch, repeat from * to end, join with a slip stitch. 120 stitches.

Round 21: Make 1 chain, * work 1 double crochet into next 19 stitches, work 2 double crochets into following stitch, repeat from * to end, join with a slip stitch. 126 stitches.

Round 22: Make 1 chain, * work 1 double crochet into next 20 stitches, work 2 double crochets into following stitch, repeat from * to end, join with a slip stitch. 132 stitches.

Round 23: Make 1 chain, * work 1 double crochet into next 21 stitches, work 2 double crochets into following stitch, repeat from * to end, join with a slip stitch. 138 stitches.

Round 24: Make 1 chain, * work 1 double crochet into next 22 stitches, work 2 double crochets into following stitch, repeat from * to end, join with a slip stitch. 144 stitches.

Round 25: Make 1 chain, * work 1 double crochet into next 23 stitches, work 2 double crochets into following stitch, repeat from * to end, join with a slip stitch. 150 stitches.

Round 26: Make 1 chain, * work 1 double crochet into next 24 stitches, work 2 double crochets into following stitch, repeat from * to end, join with a slip stitch. 156 stitches.

Round 27: Make 1 chain, work 1 double crochet into each stitch to end working through the back loop only, join with a slip stitch.

Rounds 28 – 39: Make 1 chain, work 1 double crochet into each stitch to end, join with a slip stitch.
Fasten off.

BALLS

Using 3mm (US C/2) hook and yarn of choice make 3 chains, join with a slip stitch into first chain made to form a ring.

Round 1: Make 1 chain, work 6 double crochets into the ring, join with a slip stitch. 6 stitches.

Round 2: Make 1 chain, work 2 double crochets into each stitch to end, join with a slip stitch. 12 stitches.

Round 3: Make 1 chain, * work 1 double crochet into next stitch, work 2 double crochets into following stitch, repeat from * to end, join with a slip stitch. 18 stitches.

Round 4: Make 1 chain, * work 1 double crochet into next 2 stitches, work 2 double crochets into next stitch, repeat from * to end, join with a slip stitch. 24 stitches.

Round 5: Make 1 chain, * work 1 double crochet into next 3 stitches, work 2 double crochets into next stitch, repeat from * to end, join with a slip stitch. 30 stitches.

Round 6: Make 1 chain, * work 1 double crochet into next 4 stitches, work 2 double crochets into next stitch, repeat from * to end, join with a slip stitch. 36 stitches.

Rounds 7 – 15: Make 1 chain, work 1 double crochet into each stitch to end, join with a slip stitch.

Round 16: Make 1 chain, * work 1 double crochet into next 4 stitches, work 2 double crochets together, repeat from * to end, join with a slip stitch. 30 stitches.

Start stuffing on round 16 and continue to stuff as you complete the decreasing.

Round 17: Make 1 chain, * work 1 double crochet into next 3 stitches, work 2 double crochets together, repeat from * to end, join with a slip stitch. 24 stitches

Round 18: Make 1 chain, * work 1 double crochet into next 2 stitches, work 2 double crochets together, repeat from * to end, join with a slip stitch. 18 stitches.

Round 19: Make 1 chain, * work 1 double crochet into next stitch, work 2 double crochets together, repeat from * to end, join with a slip stitch. 12 stitches.

Round 20: Make 1 chain, work 2 double crochets together to end. 6 stitches.

MAKING UP

Cut yarn leaving a tail long enough to sew up, using a tapestry needle use a running stitch through the top of the remaining 6 stitches, pull tight to secure.

HOW TO PLAY

Simply mix up all of the coloured balls on a table, and see if your child can match the correct coloured ball with the corresponding basket.

NUMBER DISKS

Help encourage your child to count with these disks. Mix them up and see if they can get them in the correct order. Be as creative with your colour combinations as you like!

SKILL LEVEL: SOME EXPERIENCE

YOU'LL NEED:

YARN
Rowan Baby Cashsoft Merino or any No.3 light weight yarn (photographed in Mint 109, Vintage Pink 105 and Apple 110)

HOOK
3mm (US C/2) hook

NUMBER DISKS

SIZE
11cm/4¼in diameter

TENSION
25 sts and 11 rows to 10cm/4in
Measured over treble crochet using 3mm (US C/2) hook.

DISKS – (MAKE 5)
Using 3mm (US C/2) hook, make 4 chains, join with a slip stitch into first chain made to form a ring.

Round 1: Make 3 chains (this counts as a treble crochet) work a further 11 treble crochets into ring. 12 stitches.

Round 2: Make 3 chains (this counts as a treble crochet) work 1 treble crochet into same stitch, work 2 double crochets into each stitch to end. 24 stitches.

Round 3: Make 3 chains (this counts as a treble crochet) * work 1 treble crochet into next stitch, work 2 treble crochets into following stitch, repeat from * to end. 36 stitches.

Round 4: Make 3 chains (this counts as a treble crochet) * work 1 treble crochet into next 2 stitches, work 2 treble crochets into following stitch, repeat from * to end. 48 stitches.

Round 5: Make 3 chains (this counts as a treble crochet) * work 1 treble crochet into next 3 stitches, work 2 treble crochets into following stitch, repeat from * to end. 60 stitches.

Round 6: Make 3 chains (this counts as a treble crochet) * work 1 treble crochet into next 4 stitches, work 2 treble crochets into following stitch, repeat from * to end, join with a slip stitch to start of round. 72 stitches. Fasten off.

NUMBER ONE
Using 3mm (US C/2) hook, make 16 chains.
Row 1: Work 1 double crochet into second

chain from hook, work 1 double crochet into each stitch to end. 15 stitches.

Row 2: Make 1 chain, work 1 double crochet into each stitch to end.

Row 3: Make 1 chain, work 1 double crochet into each stitch to end.
Fasten off.

NUMBER TWO

Using 3mm (US C/2) hook, make 4 chains.

Row 1: Work 1 double crochet into second chain from hook, work 1 half treble crochet into the next stitch, work 1 treble crochet into the following stitch. 3 stitches.

Row 2: Make 2 chains, work 1 treble crochet into the first stitch, work 1 half treble crochet into the next stitch, work 1 double crochet into the last stitch.

Row 3: Make 1 chain, work 1 double crochet into the first stitch, work half treble crochet into the next stitch, work 1 treble crochet into the last stitch.

Row 4: Make 2 chains, work 1 treble crochet into the first stitch, work 1 half treble crochet into the next stitch, work 1 double crochet into the last stitch.

Row 5: Make 1 chain, work 1 double crochet into each stitch to end.

Row 6: Make 1 chain, work 1 double crochet into each stitch to end.

Row 7: Make 1 chain, work 1 double crochet into the first stitch, work half treble crochet into the next stitch, work 1 treble crochet into the last stitch.

Row 8: Make 2 chains, work 1 treble crochet into the first stitch, work 1 half treble crochet into the next stitch, work 1 double crochet into the last stitch.

Row 9: Make 1 chain, work 1 double crochet into the first stitch, work half treble crochet into the next stitch, work 1 treble crochet into the last stitch.

Row 10: Make 2 chains, work 1 treble crochet into the first stitch, work 1 half treble crochet into the next stitch, work 1 double crochet into the last stitch.

Row 11: Make 1 chain, work 1 double crochet into the first stitch, work half treble crochet into the next stitch, work 1 treble crochet into the last stitch.

Row 12: Make 2 chains, work 1 treble crochet into the first stitch, work 1 half treble crochet into the next stitch, work 1 double crochet into the last stitch.

Row 13: Make 1 chain, work 1 double crochet into the first stitch, work half treble crochet into the next stitch, work 1 treble crochet into the last stitch.

Row 14: Make 2 chains, work 1 treble crochet into the first stitch, work 1 half treble crochet into the next stitch, work 1 double crochet into the last stitch.

Row 15: Make 1 chain, work 1 double crochet into each stitch to end.

Row 16: Make 1 chain, work 1 double crochet into each stitch to end.

Row 17: Make 1 chain, work 1 double crochet into each stitch to end.

Row 18: Make 1 chain, work 1 double crochet into the first stitch, work half treble crochet into the next stitch, work 1 treble crochet into the last stitch.

Row 19: Make 2 chains, work 1 treble crochet into the first stitch, work 1 half treble crochet into the next stitch, work 1 double crochet into the last stitch.

Row 20: Make 1 chain, work 1 double crochet into the first stitch, work half treble crochet into the next stitch, work 1 treble crochet into the last stitch.

Row 21: Make 2 chains, work 1 treble crochet into the first stitch, work 1 half treble crochet into the next stitch, work 1 double crochet into the last stitch, make 9 chains.

Row 22: Work 1 double crochet into second chain from hook, work 1 double crochet into each stitch to end. 11 stitches.

Row 23: Make 1 chain, work 1 double crochet into each stitch to end.

Row 24: Make 1 chain, work 1 double crochet into each stitch to end.
Fasten off.

NUMBER THREE

Using 3mm (US C/2) hook, make 12 chains.

Row 1: Work 1 double crochet into the second stitch from hook, work 1 double crochet into each stitch to end. 11 stitches.

Row 2: Make 1 chain, work 1 double crochet into each stitch to end.

Row 3: Make 1 chain, work 1 double crochet into each stitch to end.

Row 4: Make 1 chain, slip stitch into the next stitch, make 2 chains, work 1 treble crochet into the next stitch, work 1 half treble crochet into the following stitch, work 1 double crochet into the next stitch, turn. 3 stitches.

Row 5: Make 1 chain, work 1 double crochet into the first stitch, work 1 half treble into the next stitch, work 1 treble into last stitch.

Row 6: Make 2 chains, work 1 treble crochet into the first stitch, work 1 half treble into the next stitch, work 1 double crochet into the last stitch.

Row 7: Make 1 chain, work 1 double crochet into each stitch to end.

Row 8: Make 1 chain, work 1 double crochet into each stitch to end.

Row 9: Make 1 chain, work 1 double crochet into each stitch, make 1 chain, work 3 slip stitches into the side of row 9, 8 and 7. 3 stitches.

Row 10: Make 2 chains, work 1 treble crochet into next stitch, work 1 half treble crochet into the following stitch, work 1 double crochet into the last stitch.

Row 11: Make 1 chain, work 1 double crochet into the first stitch, work 1 half treble crochet into the next stitch, work 1 treble crochet into the last stitch.

Row 12: Make 2 chains, work 1 treble crochet into next stitch, work 1 half treble crochet into the following stitch, work 1 double crochet into the last stitch.

Row 13: Make 1 chain, work 1 double crochet into the first stitch, work 1 half treble crochet into the next stitch, work 1 treble crochet into the last stitch.

Row 14: Make 2 chains, work 1 treble crochet into next stitch, work 1 half treble crochet into the following stitch, work 1 double crochet into the last stitch.

Row 15: Make 1 chain, work 1 double crochet into the first stitch, work 1 half treble crochet into the next stitch, work 1 treble crochet into the last stitch.

Row 16: Make 1 chain, work 1 double crochet into each stitch to end.

Row 17: Make 1 chain, work 1 double crochet into each stitch to end.

Row 18: Make 1 chain, work 1 double crochet into each stitch to end.

Row 19: Make 1 chain, work 1 double crochet into the first stitch, work 1 half treble crochet into the next stitch, work 1 treble into the last stitch.

Row 20: Make 2 chains, work 1 treble crochet into last stitch, work 1 half treble into the next stitch, work 1 double crochet into the last stitch.

Row 21: Make 1 chain, work 1 double crochet into the first stitch, work 1 half treble crochet into the next stitch, work 1 treble crochet into the last stitch.

Row 22: Make 2 chains, work 1 treble

crochet into last stitch, work 1 half treble into the next stitch, work 1 double crochet into the last stitch.
Fasten off.

NUMBER FOUR

Using 3mm (US C/2) hook, make 9 chains.
Row 1: Work 1 double crochet into the second chain from hook, work 1 double crochet into each stitch to end. 8 stitches.
Row 2: Make 1 chain, work 1 double crochet into each stitch to end.
Row 3: Make 1 chain, work 1 double crochet into each stitch to end.
Row 4: Make 1 chain, work 1 double crochet into the next 3 stitches, turn. 3 stitches.
Row 5: Make 1 chain, work 1 double crochet into each stitch to end.
Row 6: Make 1 chain, work 1 double crochet into each stitch to end.
Row 7: Make 1 chain, work 1 double crochet into each stitch to end.
Row 8: Make 1 chain, work 1 double crochet into each stitch, make 6 chains, turn. 9 stitches.
Row 9: Work 1 double crochet into second stitch from hook, work 1 double crochet into next 8 stitches, make 7 chains. 16 stitches.
Row 10: Work 1 double crochet into the second stitch from hook, work 1 double crochet into each stitch to end. 15 stitches.
Row 11: Make 1 chain, work 1 double crochet into each stitch to end.
Row 12: Make 1 chain, work 1 double crochet into each stitch to end.
Fasten off.

NUMBER FIVE

Using 3mm (US C/2) hook , make 12 chains.
Row 1: Work 1 double crochet into the second chain from hook, work 1 double crochet into each stitch to end. 11 stitches.
Row 2: Make 1 chain, work 1 double crochet into each stitch to end.
Row 3: Make 1 chain, work 1 double crochet into each stitch to end.
Row 4: Make 1 chain, work 1 double crochet into the next 3 stitches, turn. 3 stitches.
Row 5: Make 1 chain, work 1 double crochet into each stitch to end.
Row 6: Make 1 chain, work 1 double crochet into the next 2 stitches, turn. 2 stitches.

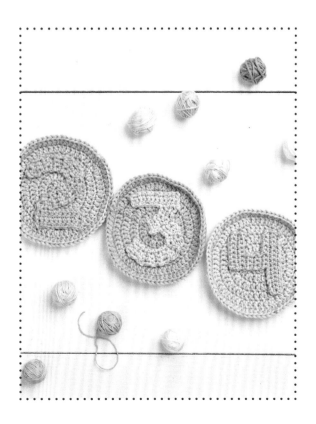

Row 7: Make 1 chain, miss the next stitch, work 1 double crochet into the next stitch. 1 stitch.

Row 8: Make 2 chains, work 1 double crochet into the chain space made on previous row, work 1 half treble crochet into the side of the last stitch on row 6, work 1 double crochet into the unworked stitch on row 5. 3 stitches.

Row 9: Make 1 chain, work 1 double crochet into the first stitch, work 1 half treble crochet into the next stitch, work 1 treble crochet into last stitch.

Row 10: Make 1 chain, work 1 double crochet into each stitch to end.

Row 11: Make 1 chain, work 1 double crochet into each stitch to end.

Row 12: Make 1 chain, work 1 double crochet into each stitch to end.

Row 13: Make 2 chains, work 1 treble crochet into the first stitch, work 1 half treble crochet into the next stitch, work 1 double crochet into last stitch.

Row 14: Make 1 chain, work 1 double crochet into the first stitch, work 1 half treble crochet into the next stitch, work 1 treble crochet into last stitch.

Row 15: Make 2 chains, work 1 treble crochet into the first stitch, work 1 half treble crochet into the next stitch, work 1 double crochet into last stitch.

Row 16: Make 1 chain, work 1 double crochet into the first stitch, work 1 half treble crochet into the next stitch, work 1 treble crochet into last stitch.

Row 17: Make 2 chains, work 1 treble crochet into the first stitch, work 1 half treble crochet into the next stitch, work 1 double crochet into last stitch.

Row 18: Make 1 chain, work 1 double crochet into the first stitch, work 1 half treble crochet into the next stitch, work 1 treble crochet into last stitch.

Row 19: Make 2 chains, work 1 treble crochet into the first stitch, work 1 half treble crochet into the next stitch, work 1 double crochet into last stitch.

Row 20: Make 1 chain, work 1 double crochet into the first stitch, work 1 half treble crochet into the next stitch, work 1 treble crochet into last stitch.

Row 21: Make 1 chain, work 1 double crochet into each stitch to end.

Row 22: Make 1 chain, work 1 double crochet into each stitch to end.

Row 23: Make 1 chain, work 1 double crochet into each stitch to end.

Row 24: Make 1 chain, work 1 double crochet into the first stitch, work 1 half treble crochet into the next stitch, work 1 treble crochet into the last stitch.

Row 25: Make 2 chains, work 1 treble crochet into first stitch, work 1 half treble into the next stitch, work 1 double crochet into the last stitch.

Row 26: Make 1 chain, work 1 double crochet into the first stitch, work 1 half treble crochet into the next stitch, work 1 treble crochet into the last stitch.

Row 27: Make 2 chains, work 1 treble crochet into first stitch, work 1 half treble into the next stitch, work 1 double crochet into the last stitch.

Fasten off.

MAKING UP

Using matching yarn to numbers and using photo as a guide, sew each number onto a disk.

FINGER PUPPETS

These lovely woodland-themed finger puppets are made from a soft Egyptian cotton.
They will bring a lot of joy to children of all ages and will be kept for years to come.

SKILL LEVEL: INTERMEDIATE

YOU'LL NEED:

YARN
Rowan Summerlite 4ply or any No.1 super
fine weight yarn

A – 1 x 50g of Langoustine 440
B – 1 x 50g of Pure White 417
C – 1 x 50g of Washed Linen 418
D – 1 x 50g of Blossom 444
E – 1 x 50g of Rooibos 441
F – 1 x 50g of Touch of Gold 439
G – 1 x 50g of Green Bay 445
H – 1 x 50g of Periwinkle 424
J – 1 x 50g of Sand Dune 438
K – 1 x 50g of Duck Egg 419

HOOK
1.75mm (US 6) hook

EXTRAS
Toy stuffing
Stitch marker
Black thread for embroidery

FINGER PUPPETS

TENSION
28 sts and 30 rows to 10cm/4in
Measured over double crochet using
1.75mm (US 6) hook.

SPECIAL INSTRUCTIONS
When changing to a different colour yarn,
work the last two loops of the previous
stitch in the new colour.

Puff stitch (this can also be known as popcorn stitch):
Yarn over hook and insert through stitch.
Pull a loop through.
Yarn over hook and pull through 2 loops on
the hook (2 loops remaining on the hook).
Yarn over hook and insert in to the same
stitch.
Pull a loop through.
Yarn over hook and pull through 2 loops
(3 loops left on hook).
Yarn over hook and insert in to same stitch.

Pull a loop through.
Yarn over hook and pull through 2 loops
(4 loops left on hook).
Yarn over hook and insert in to same stitch.
Pull a loop through.
Yarn over hook and pull through 2 loops
(5 loops left on hook).
Yarn over hook and pull through all 5 loops
on hook.

BASIC SHAPES
FINGER COVER
Using 1.75mm (US 6) hook and yarn
indicated, make a magic ring.
Round 1: Work 6 double crochets into the
ring. 6 stitches.
Round 2: * Work 1 double crochet into
next stitch, work 2 double crochets into next
stitch, repeat from * to end. 9 stitches.
Round 3: * Work 1 double crochet into next
2 stitches, work 2 double crochets into next
stitch, repeat from * to end. 12 stitches.

Round 4: * Work 1 double crochet into next 3 stitches, work 2 double crochets into next stitch, repeat from * to end. 15 stitches.

Round 5: * Work 1 double crochet into next 4 stitches, work 2 double crochets into next stitch, repeat from * to end. 18 stitches.

Round 6: Work 1 double crochet into each stitch.

Rounds 7 – 21: As round 6. Fasten off.

HEAD

Using 1.75mm (US 6) hook and yarn indicated, make a magic ring.

Round 1: Work 5 double crochets into the ring. 5 stitches.

Round 2: * Work 2 double crochets into next stitch, repeat from * to end. 10 stitches.

Round 3: * Work 1 double crochet into next stitch, work 2 double crochets into next stitch, repeat from * to end. 15 stitches.

Round 4: * Work 1 double crochet into next 2 stitches, work 2 double crochets into next stitch, repeat from * to end. 20 stitches.

Round 5: * Work 1 double crochet into next 3 stitches, work 2 double crochets into next stitch, repeat from * to end. 25 stitches.

Round 6: Work 1 double crochet into each stitch.

Rounds 7 – 10: As round 6.

Round 11: * Work 1 double crochet into next 3 stitches, work 2 double crochets together, repeat from * to end. 20 stitches.

Round 12: * Work 1 double crochet into next 2 stitches, work 2 double crochets together, repeat from * to end. 15 stitches. Start to stuff and continue as you work.

Round 13: * Work 1 double crochet into next stitch, work 2 double crochets together, repeat from * to end. 10 stitches.

Round 14: * Work 2 double crochets

together, repeat from * to end. 5 stitches. Fasten off leaving a long length of yarn.

MAKING UP

Work a running stitch around last round and pull tight to close.

HOOD

Using 1.75mm (US 6) hook and yarn indicated, make a magic ring.

Round 1: Work 5 double crochets into the ring. 5 stitches.

Round 2: * Work 2 double crochets into next stitch, repeat from * to end. 10 stitches.

Round 3: * Work 1 double crochet into next stitch, work 2 double crochets into next stitch, repeat from * to end. 15 stitches.

Round 4: * Work 1 double crochet into next 2 stitches, work 2 double crochets into next stitch, repeat from * to end. 20 stitches.

Round 5: * Work 1 double crochet into next 3 stitches, work 2 double crochets into next stitch, repeat from * to end. 25 stitches.

Round 6: Work 1 double crochet into each stitch.

Rounds 7 – 12: As round 6.**

BELLY

Using 1.75mm (US 6) hook and yarn indicated, make 9 chains.

Row 1: Working into back loop only, work 1 double crochet into second chain from hook, work 1 double crochet into next 6 stitches, work 3 double crochets into last stitch, **do not turn.**

Working into the opposite side of starting chain, proceed in rounds as follows:

Round 1: Work 1 double crochet into next 6 stitches, work 2 double crochets into last stitch. 18 stitches.

Round 2: Work 2 double crochets into next

stitch, work 1 double crochet into next 6 stitches, (work 2 double crochets into next stitch) 3 times, work 1 double crochet into next 6 stitches, (work 2 double crochets into next stitch) twice. 24 stitches.

Fasten off leaving a long length of yarn.

FOX

Make head using yarn B.
Make finger cover using yarn A.
Make belly using yarn B.
Make hood using yarn A, **do not break yarn.**

NOSE

Place a stitch marker on the last stitch made on the hood. Continue working on from the hood in rows as follows:

Row 1: Make 1 chain, work 1 double crochet into next 10 stitches, turn. 10 stitches.

Row 2: Make 1 chain, work 2 double crochets together, work 1 double crochet into next 6 stitches, work 2 double crochets together, turn. 8 stitches.

Row 3: Make 1 chain, work 2 double crochets together, work 1 double crochet into next 4 stitches, work 2 double crochets together, turn. 6 stitches.

Row 4: Make 1 chain, work 2 double crochets together, work 1 double crochet into next 2 stitches, work 2 double crochets together, turn. 4 stitches.

Row 5: Make 1 chain, (work 2 double crochets together) twice, turn. 2 stitches.

Row 6: Make 1 chain, work 1 double crochet into each stitch, turn.

Row 7: Make 1 chain, work 2 double crochets together, turn. 1 stitch.

Row 8: Make 1 chain, work 1 double crochet into next stitch.

Fasten off leaving a long length of yarn.

Rejoin yarn A to point marked by stitch marker.

Next Row: Work a slip stitch onto side of nose, work double crochets up to tip of nose, work 3 double crochets into tip of nose, work double crochets down side of nose, join with a slip stitch to hood.

EARS – (MAKE 2)

Using 1.75mm (US 6) hook and yarn A, make a magic ring.

Round 1: Work 4 double crochets into the ring. 4 stitches.

Round 2: * Work 1 double crochet into next stitch, work 2 double crochets into next stitch, repeat from * to end. 6 stitches.

Round 3: * Work 1 double crochet into next 2 stitches, work 2 double crochets into next stitch, repeat from * to end. 8 stitches.

Round 4: * Work 1 double crochet into next 3 stitches, work 2 double crochets into next

stitch, repeat from * to end. 10 stitches.
Round 5: * Work 1 double crochet into next 4 stitches, work 2 double crochets into next stitch, repeat from * to end. 12 stitches.
Round 6: * Work 1 double crochet into next 5 stitches, work 2 double crochets into next stitch, repeat from * to end. 14 stitches.
Fasten off leaving a long length of yarn.

TAIL

Using 1.75mm (US 6) hook and yarn B, make a magic ring.
Round 1: Work 4 double crochets into the ring. 4 stitches.
Round 2: * Work 1 double crochet into next stitch, work 2 double crochets into next stitch, repeat from * to end. 6 stitches.
Round 3: * Work 1 double crochet into next 2 stitches, work 2 double crochets into next stitch, repeat from * to end. 8 stitches.
Change to yarn A.
Round 4: * Work 1 double crochet into next 3 stitches, work 2 double crochets into next stitch, repeat from * to end. 10 stitches.
Round 5: Work 1 double crochet into each stitch.
Round 6: * Work 1 double crochet into next 3 stitches, work 2 double crochets together, repeat from * to end. 8 stitches.
Round 7: As round 5.
Round 8: * Work 1 double crochet into next 2 stitches, work 2 double crochets together, repeat from * to end. 6 stitches.
Round 9: As round 5.
Fasten off leaving a long length of yarn.

MAKING UP

Use black thread to embroider nose and eyes, using a single strand of thread to embroider eyebrows 1 round above eyes. Using yarn B embroider 3 lines on inner ear

to form a W shape, sew ears onto hood. Sew hood to head. Sew head to finger cover. Sew belly to lower half of finger cover. Close hole in tail and attach tail to finger cover a few rows from base.

RABBIT

Make head using yarn B.
Make finger cover using yarn C.
Make belly using yarn B.
Make hood using yarn C.

EARS – (MAKE 2)

Using 1.75mm (US 6) hook and yarn C, make a magic ring.
Round 1: Work 4 double crochets into the ring. 4 stitches.
Round 2: * Work 1 double crochet into next stitch, work 2 double crochets into next stitch, repeat from * to end. 6 stitches.
Round 3: * Work 1 double crochet into next 2 stitches, work 2 double crochets into next stitch, repeat from * to end. 8 stitches.
Round 4: * Work 1 double crochet into next

3 stitches, work 2 double crochets into next stitch, repeat from * to end. 10 stitches.

Round 5: * Work 1 double crochet into next 4 stitches, work 2 double crochets into next stitch, repeat from * to end. 12 stitches.

Round 6: Work 1 double crochet into each stitch.

Round 7: As round 6.

Round 8: * Work 2 double crochets together, repeat from * to end. 6 stitches.
Fasten off leaving a long length of yarn.

TAIL

Using 1.75mm (US 6) hook and yarn C, make a magic ring.

Round 1: Work 5 double crochets into the ring. 5 stitches.

Round 2: * Work 2 double crochets into next stitch, repeat from * to end. 10 stitches.

Round 3: Work 1 double crochet into next stitch.

Round 4: As round 3.

Round 5: * Work 2 double crochets together, repeat from * to end. 5 stitches.
Fasten off leaving a long length of yarn.

MAKING UP

Use black thread to embroider eyes centrally with 6 stitches visible between them. Use a single strand of thread to embroider eyebrows 1 round above eyes. Using yarn D, embroider nose between eyes. Sew a running stitch around last round of ears to close. Pass yarn through centre of ear and through centre of magic ring, then fold ear flat. Using yarn D, embroider 3 lines on inner ear at the bottom fanning outwards (see photo). Sew ears onto hood. Sew hood to head. Sew head to finger cover. Sew belly to lower half of finger cover. Stuff tail lightly and attach tail to finger cover a few rows from base.

HEDGEHOG ON TOADSTOOL

Make finger cover using yarn B.

TOADSTOOL HEAD

Using 1.75mm (US 6) hook and yarn E, make a magic ring.

Round 1: Work 6 double crochets into the ring. 6 stitches.

Round 2: * Work 1 double crochet into next stitch, work 2 double crochets into next stitch, repeat from * to end. 9 stitches.

Round 3: * Work 1 double crochet into next 2 stitches, work 2 double crochets into next stitch, repeat from * to end. 12 stitches.

Round 4: * Work 1 double crochet into next 3 stitches, work 2 double crochets into next stitch, repeat from * to end. 15 stitches.

Round 5: * Work 1 double crochet into next 4 stitches, work 2 double crochets into next stitch, repeat from * to end. 18 stitches.

Round 6: * Work 1 double crochet into next 5 stitches, work 2 double crochets into next stitch, repeat from * to end. 21 stitches.

Round 7: * Work 1 double crochet into next 6 stitches, work 2 double crochets into next

stitch, repeat from * to end. 24 stitches.

Round 8: * Work 1 double crochet into next 7 stitches, work 2 double crochets into next stitch, repeat from * to end. 27 stitches.

Round 9: * Work 1 double crochet into next 8 stitches, work 2 double crochets into next stitch, repeat from * to end. 30 stitches.

Round 10: Work 1 double crochet into each stitch.

Round 11: As round 10.

Fasten off leaving a long length of yarn.

HEDGEHOG

Using 1.75mm (US 6) hook and yarn B, make a magic ring.

Round 1: Work 4 double crochets into the ring. 4 stitches.

Round 2: * Work 1 double crochet into next stitch, work 2 double crochets into next stitch, repeat from * to end. 6 stitches.

Round 3: Work 1 double crochet into next 2 stitches, work 2 double crochets into next 3 stitches, work 1 double crochet into next stitch. 9 stitches.

Round 4: Work 1 double crochet into next 4 stitches, work 2 double crochets into next 4 stitches, work 1 double crochet into next stitch. 13 stitches.

Round 5: Work 1 double crochet into next 4 stitches, (work 1 double crochet into next stitch, work 2 double crochets into next stitch) 4 times, work 1 double crochet into next stitch. 17 stitches.

Round 6: Work 1 double crochet into next 7 stitches, (work 1 double crochet into next 2 stitches, work 2 double crochets into next stitch) 3 times, work 1 double crochet into next stitch. 20 stitches.

Change to yarn F.

Round 7: * Work 1 double crochet into next stitch, work 1 puff into next stitch, repeat from * to end.

Round 8: Work 1 double crochet into next 2 stitches, * work 1 puff into next stitch, work 1 double crochet into next stitch, repeat from * to end.

Round 9: Work 1 puff into next stitch, work 1 double crochet into next 2 stitches, * work 1 puff into next stitch, work 1 double crochet into next stitch, repeat from * to last stitch, work 1 puff into next stitch. Start to stuff, and continue stuffing as you work.

Round 10: Work 2 double crochets together, work 1 puff into next stitch, work 2 double crochets together, work 1 double crochet into next stitch, work 1 puff into next stitch, (work 2 double crochets together, work 1 double crochet into next stitch, work 1 puff into next stitch) 3 times, work 1 double crochet into next stitch. 15 stitches.

Round 11: Work 2 double crochets together, work 1 puff into next stitch, (work 2 double crochets together) twice, work 1 puff into next stitch, work 2 double crochets together, work 1 puff into next stitch, work 1 double crochet into next stitch, work 1 puff into next stitch, work 2 double crochets together. 10 stitches.

Round 12: * Work 2 double crochets together, repeat from * to end. 5 stitches. Fasten off leaving a long length of yarn, pass this yarn through body to base of hedgehog.

MAKING UP

Use yarn B to embroider spots onto toadstool head. Place toadstool head onto finger cover, sew hedgehog to finger cover, passing through toadstool head to secure both. Use black thread to embroider eyes onto hedgehog over round 4 with 3 stitches visible between them, using a single strand of thread to embroider eyebrows 1 round above eyes. Using yarn D embroider nose between eyes. Using yarn G embroider blades of grass and flower stems around base of finger cover. Using yarn H embroider inverted Vs to represent bluebells on flower stems.

OWL IN TREE

Make head using yarn K.
Make finger cover using yarn J.

TREE

Using 1.75mm (US 6) hook and yarn G, make a magic ring.
Round 1: Work 6 double crochets into the ring. 6 stitches.
Round 2: * Work 1 double crochet into next stitch, work 2 double crochets into next stitch, repeat from * to end. 9 stitches.
Round 3: * Work 1 double crochet into next 2 stitches, work 2 double crochets into next stitch, repeat from * to end. 12 stitches.
Round 4: * Work 1 double crochet into next 3 stitches, work 2 double crochets into next stitch, repeat from * to end. 15 stitches.
Round 5: * Work 1 double crochet into next 4 stitches, work 2 double crochets into next stitch, repeat from * to end. 18 stitches.
Round 6: * Work 1 double crochet into next 5 stitches, work 2 double crochets into next stitch, repeat from * to end. 21 stitches.
Round 7: * Work 1 double crochet into next 6 stitches, work 2 double crochets into next stitch, repeat from * to end. 24 stitches.
Round 8: * Work 1 double crochet into next 7 stitches, work 2 double crochets into next stitch, repeat from * to end. 27 stitches.
Round 9: * Work 1 double crochet into next 8 stitches, work 2 double crochets into next stitch, repeat from * to end. 30 stitches.
Round 10: Work 1 double crochet into each stitch.
Rounds 11 – 15: As round 10.
Fasten off leaving a long length of yarn.

EYES – (MAKE 2)

Using 1.75mm (US 6) hook and yarn B, make a magic ring.
Round 1: Work 6 double crochets into the ring. 6 stitches.
Round 2: * Work 2 double crochets into each stitch, repeat from * to end. 12 stitches.
Fasten off leaving a long length of yarn.

WINGS – (MAKE 2)

Using 1.75mm (US 6) hook and yarn G, make a magic ring.
Round 1: Work 3 double crochets into the ring. 3 stitches.
Proceed in rows as follows:
Row 1: Make 1 chain, * work 2 double crochets into each stitch, repeat from * to end, turn. 6 stitches.
Row 2: Make 1 chain, * work 1 double

crochet into next stitch, work 2 double crochets into next stitch, repeat from * to end, turn. 9 stitches.

Row 3: Make 1 chain, * work 1 double crochet into next 2 stitches, work 2 double crochets into next stitch, repeat from * to end. 12 stitches.

Fasten off leaving a long length of yarn.

MAKING UP

Use yarns A and E to embroider spots onto V shaped leaves onto tree. Using black thread, embroider a semi-circular line across 4 stitches between rounds 1 and 2 of eyes. Sew eyes to head so they touch centrally. Sew wings to each side of head with top of wings level with top of eyes. Using yarn F embroider a small beak centrally between eyes. Place tree onto finger cover, sew owl to finger cover, passing through tree to secure both.

SUPER SOFT BALL

Perfect for all children, these super soft but durable balls can be made in different sizes. For smaller children use a lighter weight stuffing. For older children, why not put dried lentils inside a sealed bag to make a heavier weight ball?

SKILL LEVEL: EASY

YOU'LL NEED:

YARN
1 x 50g of Rowan Summerlite DK or any
No.3 light weight yarn
(small ball photographed in Pear 463 (A),
large ball photographed in Seashell 466 (B))

HOOK
3.5mm (US E/4) hook

EXTRAS
Toy stuffing

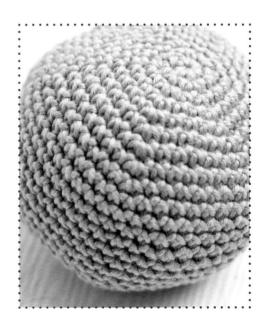

SUPER SOFT BALL

SIZE

Approx. circumference:
Small – 22.5cm/8¾in
Medium – 35cm/13¾in

TENSION

24 sts and 22 rows to 10cm/4in
Measured over double crochet using 3.5mm
(US E/4) hook.

SMALL BALL

Using 3.5mm (US E/4) hook and yarn A
make a magic loop, work 6 double crochets
into the loop. 6 stitches.

Round 1: Work 2 double crochets into each
stitch from previous round. 12 stitches.

Round 2: * Work 1 double crochet into
next stitch, work 2 double crochets into next
stitch, repeat from * to end of round. 18
stitches.

Round 3: * Work 1 double crochet into next
2 stitches, work 2 double crochets into

next stitch, repeat from * to end of round.
24 stitches.

Round 4: * Work 1 double crochet into next
3 stitches, work 2 double crochets into next
stitch, repeat from * to end of round. 30
stitches.

Round 5: * Work 1 double crochet into next
4 stitches, work 2 double crochets into next
stitch, repeat from * to end of round. 36
stitches.

Round 6: * Work 1 double crochet into next
5 stitches, work 2 double crochets into next
stitch, repeat from * to end of round. 42
stitches.

Round 7: * Work 1 double crochet into next
6 stitches, work 2 double crochets into next
stitch, repeat from * to end of round. 48
stitches.

Round 8: * Work 1 double crochet into next
7 stitches, work 2 double crochets into next
stitch, repeat from * to end of round.
54 stitches.

Rounds 9 – 17: Work 1 double crochet into each stitch to end of round.

Round 18: * Work 1 double crochet into next 7 stitches, double crochet 2 stitches together, repeat from * to end of round. 48 stitches.

Round 19: * Work 1 double crochet into next 6 stitches, double crochet 2 stitches together, repeat from * to end of round. 42 stitches.

Round 20: * Work 1 double crochet into next 5 stitches, double crochet 2 stitches together, repeat from * to end of round. 36 stitches.

Round 21: * Work 1 double crochet into next 4 stitches, double crochet 2 stitches together, repeat from * to end of round. 30 stitches.

Round 22: * Work 1 double crochet into next 3 stitches, double crochet 2 stitches together, repeat from * to end of round. 24 stitches.

Round 23: * Work 1 double crochet into next 2 stitches, double crochet 2 stitches together, repeat from * to end of round. 18 stitches.

Round 24: * Work 1 double crochet into next stitch, double crochet 2 stitches together, repeat from * to end of round. 12 stitches.

Round 25: * Double crochet 2 stitches together, repeat from * to end of round. 6 stitches.
Fasten off.

LARGE BALL

Using 3.5mm (US E/4) hook and yarn B make a magic loop, work 6 double crochets into the loop. 6 stitches.

Round 1: Work 2 double crochets into each stitch from previous round. 12 stitches.

Round 2: * Work 1 double crochet into next stitch, work 2 double crochets into next stitch, repeat from * to end of round. 18 stitches.

Round 3: * Work 1 double crochet into next 2 stitches, work 2 double crochets into next stitch, repeat from * to end of round. 24 stitches.

Round 4: * Work 1 double crochet into next 3 stitches, work 2 double crochets into next stitch, repeat from * to end of round. 30 stitches.

Round 5: * Work 1 double crochet into next 4 stitches, work 2 double crochets into next stitch, repeat from * to end of round. 36 stitches.

Round 6: * Work 1 double crochet into next 5 stitches, work 2 double crochets into next stitch, repeat from * to end of round. 42 stitches.

Round 7: * Work 1 double crochet into next 6 stitches, work 2 double crochets into next stitch, repeat from * to end of round. 48 stitches.

Round 8: * Work 1 double crochet into next 7 stitches, work 2 double crochets into next stitch, repeat from * to end of round. 54 stitches.

Round 9: * Work 1 double crochet into next 8 stitches, work 2 double crochets into next stitch, repeat from * to end of round. 60 stitches.

Round 10: * Work 1 double crochet into next 9 stitches, work 2 double crochets into next stitch, repeat from * to end of round. 66 stitches.

Round 11: * Work 1 double crochet into next 10 stitches, work 2 double crochets into next stitch, repeat from * to end of round. 72 stitches.

Round 12: * Work 1 double crochet into next 11 stitches, work 2 double crochets into next stitch, repeat from * to end of round. 78 stitches.

Round 13: * Work 1 double crochet into next 12 stitches, work 2 double crochets into next stitch, repeat from * to end of round. 84 stitches.

Rounds 14 – 23: Work 1 double crochet into each stitch to end of round.

Round 24: * Work 1 double crochet into next 12 stitches, double crochet 2 stitches together, repeat from * to end of round. 78 stitches.

Round 25: * Work 1 double crochet into next 11 stitches, double crochet 2 stitches together, repeat from * to end of round. 72 stitches.

Round 26: * Work 1 double crochet into next 10 stitches, double crochet 2 stitches together, repeat from * to end of round. 66 stitches.

Round 27: * Work 1 double crochet into next 9 stitches, double crochet 2 stitches together, repeat from * to end of round. 60 stitches.

Round 28: * Work 1 double crochet into next 8 stitches, double crochet 2 stitches together, repeat from * to end of round. 54 stitches.

Round 29: * Work 1 double crochet into next 7 stitches, double crochet 2 stitches together, repeat from * to end of round. 48 stitches.

Round 30: * Work 1 double crochet into next 6 stitches, double crochet 2 stitches together, repeat from * to end of round. 42 stitches.

Round 31: * Work 1 double crochet into next 5 stitches, double crochet 2 stitches together, repeat from * to end of round. 36 stitches.

Round 32: * Work 1 double crochet into next 4 stitches, double crochet 2 stitches together, repeat from * to end of round. 30 stitches.

Round 33: * Work 1 double crochet into next 3 stitches, double crochet 2 stitches together, repeat from * to end of round. 24 stitches.

Round 34: * Work 1 double crochet into next 2 stitches, double crochet 2 stitches together, repeat from * to end of round. 18 stitches.

Round 35: * Work 1 double crochet into next 1 stitch, double crochet 2 stitches together, repeat from * to end of round. 12 stitches.

Round 36: * Double crochet 2 stitches together, repeat from * to end of round. 6 stitches.
Fasten off.

MAKING UP
Stuff ball with toy stuffing until firm.
Cut yarn and thread through top of 6 stitches, pull tightly to secure and fasten off.

SKITTLES

A great game to play indoors and out. Simply stand the skittles and see if you can knock them down in one! Made from a medium weight cotton, these skittles are worked in the round with a band of colour worked in the middle.

SKILL LEVEL: SOME EXPERIENCE

YOU'LL NEED:

YARN
Main shade
A – 5 x 50g of Rowan Hand Knit Cotton in Ecru 251
Contrast shades
B – 1 x 50g of Rowan Hand Knit Cotton in Celery 309
C – 1 x 50g of Ballet Pink 372
D – 1 x 50g of Cloud 345
E – 1 x 50g of Feather 373
F – 1 x 50g of Sea Foam 352
G – 1 x 50g of Ice Water 239

HOOK
3mm (US C/2) hook

EXTRAS
Toy stuffing

SKITTLES

SIZE

Bowling pins – 8cm/3in diameter and
22cm/8½in high
Balls – 9cm/3½in in diameter

TENSION

19 sts and 23 rows to 10cm/4in
Measured over double crochet using 3mm
(US C/2) hook.

BOWLING PIN (MAKE 6 – 1 WITH EACH CONTRAST COLOUR)

BODY

Using 3mm (US C/2) hook and yarn A make
a magic ring.
Round 1: Work 6 double crochets into the
ring. 6 stitches.
Round 2: Work 2 double crochets into each
stitch to end. 12 stitches.
Round 3: * Work 1 double crochet into next
stitch, work 2 double crochets into following

stitch, repeat from * to end. 18 stitches.
Round 4: * Work 1 double crochet into
next 2 stitches, work 2 double crochets into
following stitch, repeat from * to end.
24 stitches.
Round 5: * Work 1 double crochet into
next 3 stitches, work 2 double crochets into
following stitch, repeat from * to end.
30 stitches.
Round 6: Work 1 double crochet into
each stitch.
Rounds 7 – 10: As round 6.
Round 11: * Work 1 double crochet into
next 3 stitches, work 2 double crochets
together, repeat from * to end. 24 stitches.
Round 12: As round 6.
Round 13: * Work 1 double crochet into
next 2 stitches, work 2 double crochets
together, repeat from * to end. 18 stitches.
Rounds 14 – 18: As round 6.
Round 19: * Work 1 double crochet into
next 2 stitches, work 2 double crochets into

following stitch, repeat from * to end.
24 stitches.
Round 20: As round 6.
Round 21: * Work 1 double crochet into next 3 stitches, work 2 double crochets into following stitch, repeat from * to end.
30 stitches.
Round 22: As round 6.
Round 23: * Work 1 double crochet into next 4 stitches, work 2 double crochets into following stitch, repeat from * to end.
36 stitches.
Round 24: As round 6.
Round 25: * Work 1 double crochet into next 5 stitches, work 2 double crochets into following stitch, repeat from * to end.
42 stitches.
Round 26: As round 6.
Round 27: * Work 1 double crochet into next 6 stitches, work 2 double crochets into following stitch, repeat from * to end.
48 stitches.
Round 28: As round 6, join with a slip stitch to next stitch.
Fasten off.
Change to contrast colour.
Rounds 29 – 35: As round 6, join with a slip stitch to next stitch.
Fasten off.
Change to yarn A.
Rounds 36 – 46: As round 6.
Round 47: * Work 1 double crochet into next 6 stitches, work 2 double crochets together, repeat from * to end. 42 stitches.
Round 48: As round 6.
Round 49: * Work 1 double crochet into next 5 stitches, work 2 double crochets together, repeat from * to end. 36 stitches.
Round 50: As round 6.
Round 51: * Work 1 double crochet into next 4 stitches, work 2 double crochets

together, repeat from * to end. 30 stitches.
Round 52: As round 6, join with a slip stitch to next stitch.
Fasten off.
Stuff firmly without overfilling, to ensure base remains flat.

BASE
Using 3mm (US C/2) hook and yarn A make a magic ring.
Round 1: Work 6 double crochets into the ring. 6 stitches.
Round 2: Work 2 double crochets into each stitch to end. 12 stitches.
Round 3: * Work 1 double crochet into next stitch, work 2 double crochets into following stitch, repeat from * to end. 18 stitches.
Round 4: * Work 1 double crochet into next 2 stitches, work 2 double crochets into following stitch, repeat from * to end.
24 stitches.
Round 5: * Work 1 double crochet into next 3 stitches, work 2 double crochets into following stitch, repeat from * to end, join with a slip stitch to next stitch, **do not fasten off**. 30 stitches.
Slip stitch to base of body.
Fasten off.

BALL
Using 3mm (US C/2) hook and contrast colour of choice, make a magic ring.
Round 1: Work 6 double crochets into the ring. 6 stitches.
Round 2: Work 2 double crochets into each stitch to end. 12 stitches.
Round 3: * Work 1 double crochet into next stitch, work 2 double crochets into following stitch, repeat from * to end. 18 stitches.
Round 4: * Work 1 double crochet into next 2 stitches, work 2 double crochets into

following stitch, repeat from * to end.
24 stitches.

Round 5: * Work 1 double crochet into next 3 stitches, work 2 double crochets into following stitch, repeat from * to end.
30 stitches.

Round 6: * Work 1 double crochet into next 4 stitches, work 2 double crochets into following stitch, repeat from * to end.
36 stitches.

Round 7: * Work 1 double crochet into next 5 stitches, work 2 double crochets into following stitch, repeat from * to end.
42 stitches.

Round 8: * Work 1 double crochet into next 6 stitches, work 2 double crochets into following stitch, repeat from * to end.
48 stitches.

Round 9: * Work 1 double crochet into next 7 stitches, work 2 double crochets into following stitch, repeat from * to end.
54 stitches.

Round 10: Work 1 double crochet into each stitch.

Rounds 11 – 18: As round 10.

Round 19: * Work 1 double crochet into next 7 stitches, work 2 double crochets together, repeat from * to end. 48 stitches.

Round 20: * Work 1 double crochet into next 6 stitches, work 2 double crochets together, repeat from * to end. 42 stitches.

Round 21: * Work 1 double crochet into next 5 stitches, work 2 double crochets together, repeat from * to end. 36 stitches.

Round 22: * Work 1 double crochet into next 4 stitches, work 2 double crochets together, repeat from * to end. 30 stitches.

Round 23: * Work 1 double crochet into next 3 stitches, work 2 double crochets together, repeat from * to end. 24 stitches.

Round 24: * Work 1 double crochet into next 2 stitches, work 2 double crochets together, repeat from * to end. 18 stitches.

Round 25: * Work 1 double crochet into next stitch, work 2 double crochets together, repeat from * to end. 12 stitches.
Begin to stuff.

Round 26: * Work 2 double crochets together, repeat from * to end. 6 stitches.
Fasten off, close hole and sew in loose ends.

CAR

Add some excitement to your children's toy box with this classic crocheted car design. Big enough for children of all ages, this will be sure to be a hit! Why not personalize your car paint work by substituting the colours?

SKILL LEVEL: SOME EXPERIENCE

YOU'LL NEED:

YARN
Deramores Studio DK or any No.3
medium weight yarn
A – 1 x 100g of Blue Velvet
B – 1 x 100g of Sky
C – 1 x 100g of Frost
D – 1 x 100g of Mist
E – 1 x 100g of Ruby
F – 1 x 100g of Ebony

HOOK
4mm (US G/6) hook

EXTRAS
Toy stuffing

CAR

SIZE
16cm/6¼in long, 9cm/3½in high, 12cm/4¾in wide

TENSION
18 sts and 19 rows to 10cm/4in
Measured over double crochet using 4mm (US G/6) hook.

SPECIAL INSTRUCTIONS
When changing to a different colour yarn, work the last two loops of the previous stitch in the new colour.

CAR BODY
Using 4mm (US G/6) hook and yarn A make a magic ring.

Row 1: Work 3 double crochets in the magic ring, turn. 3 stitches.

Row 2: Make 1 chain, work 2 double crochets into each stitch to end, turn. 6 stitches.

Row 3: Make 1 chain, * work 1 double crochet into next stitch, work 2 double crochets into following stitch, repeat from * to end, turn. 9 stitches.

Row 4: Make 1 chain, * work 1 double crochet into next 2 stitches, work 2 double crochets into following stitch, repeat from * to end, turn. 12 stitches.

Row 5: Make 1 chain, * work 1 double crochet into next 3 stitches, work 2 double crochets into following stitch, repeat from * to end, turn. 15 stitches.

Row 6: Make 1 chain, * work 1 double crochet into next 4 stitches, work 2 double crochets into following stitch, repeat from * to end, turn. 18 stitches.

Row 7: Make 1 chain, * work 1 double crochet into next 5 stitches, work 2 double crochets into following stitch, repeat from * to end, turn. 21 stitches.

Row 8: Make 1 chain, * work 1 double crochet into next 6 stitches, work 2 double crochets into following stitch, repeat from * to end, turn. 24 stitches.

Row 9: Make 1 chain, * work 1 double crochet into next 7 stitches, work 2 double crochets into following stitch, repeat from * to end, turn. 27 stitches.

Row 10: Make 1 chain, * work 1 double crochet into next 8 stitches, work 2 double crochets into following stitch, repeat from * to end, turn. 30 stitches.

Row 11: Make 1 chain, * work 1 double crochet into next 9 stitches, work 2 double crochets into following stitch, repeat from * to end, turn. 33 stitches.

Row 12: Make 1 chain, * work 1 double crochet into next 10 stitches, work 2 double crochets into following stitch, repeat from * to end, turn. 36 stitches.

Row 13: Make 1 chain, * work 1 double crochet into next 11 stitches, work 2 double crochets into following stitch, repeat from * to end, turn. 39 stitches.

Row 14: Make 1 chain, * work 1 double crochet into next 12 stitches, work 2 double crochets into following stitch, repeat from * to end, turn. 42 stitches.

Row 15: Make 1 chain, * work 1 double crochet into next 13 stitches, work 2 double crochets into following stitch, repeat from * to end, turn. 45 stitches.

Row 16: Make 1 chain, * work 1 double crochet into next 14 stitches, work 2 double crochets into following stitch, repeat from * to end, turn. 48 stitches.

Row 17: Make 1 chain, * work 1 double crochet into next 15 stitches, work 2 double crochets into following stitch, repeat from * to end, **do not turn**. 51 stitches.

Next Row: Work 1 double crochet into the end of each row of double crochets. 32 stitches.

Join with a slip stitch to the first stitch of the previous round. 83 stitches.

Proceed in rounds as follows:

Round 1: Make 1 chain, work 1 double crochet into each stitch, join with a slip stitch. 83 stitches.

Round 2: As round 1.

Round 3: Make 1 chain, work 1 double crochet into next 35 stitches, change to yarn C, work 1 double crochet into next 6 stitches, change to yarn A, work 1 double crochet into next 42 stitches, join with a slip stitch.

Round 4: Make 1 chain, work 1 double crochet into next 34 stitches, change to yarn C, work 1 double crochet into next 7 stitches, change to yarn A, work 1 double crochet into next 42 stitches, join with a slip stitch.

Round 5: Make 1 chain, work 1 double crochet into next 9 stitches, change to yarn C, work 1 double crochet into next 5 stitches, change to yarn A, work 1 double crochet into next 20 stitches, change to yarn C, work 1 double crochet into next 7 stitches, change to yarn A, work 1 double crochet into next 42 stitches, join with a slip stitch.

Rounds 6 – 15: As round 5.

Round 16: Make 1 chain, work 1 double crochet into next 34 stitches, change to yarn C, work 1 double crochet into next 7 stitches, change to yarn A, work 1 double crochet into next 42 stitches, join with a slip stitch.

Round 17: Make 1 chain, work 1 double crochet into next 35 stitches, change to yarn C, work 1 double crochet into next 6 stitches, change to yarn A, work 1 double crochet into next 42 stitches, join with a slip stitch.

Round 18: Make 1 chain, work 1 double crochet into each stitch, join with a slip stitch. 83 stitches.

Proceed in rows as follows:

Row 1: Make 1 chain, * work 1 double crochet into next 15 stitches, work 2 double crochets together, repeat from * 3 times, turn. 48 stitches.

Row 2: Make 1 chain, * work 1 double crochet into next 14 stitches, work 2 double crochets together, repeat from * to end, turn. 45 stitches.

Row 3: Make 1 chain, * work 1 double crochet into next 13 stitches, work 2 double crochets together, repeat from * to end, turn. 42 stitches.

Row 4: Make 1 chain, * work 1 double crochet into next 12 stitches, work 2 double crochets together, repeat from * to end, turn. 39 stitches.

Row 5: Make 1 chain, * work 1 double crochet into next 11 stitches, work 2 double crochets together, repeat from * to end, turn. 36 stitches.

Row 6: Make 1 chain, * work 1 double crochet into next 10 stitches, work 2 double crochets together, repeat from * to end, turn. 33 stitches.

Row 7: Make 1 chain, * work 1 double crochet into next 9 stitches, work 2 double crochets together, repeat from * to end, turn. 30 stitches.

Row 8: Make 1 chain, * work 1 double crochet into next 8 stitches, work 2 double crochets together, repeat from * to end, turn. 27 stitches.

Row 9: Make 1 chain, * work 1 double crochet into next 7 stitches, work 2 double crochets together, repeat from * to end, turn. 24 stitches.

Row 10: Make 1 chain, * work 1 double crochet into next 6 stitches, work 2 double crochets together, repeat from * to end, turn. 21 stitches.

Row 11: Make 1 chain, * work 1 double crochet into next 5 stitches, work 2 double crochets together, repeat from * to end, turn. 18 stitches.

Row 12: Make 1 chain, * work 1 double crochet into next 4 stitches, work 2 double crochets together, repeat from * to end, turn. 15 stitches.

Row 13: Make 1 chain, * work 1 double crochet into next 3 stitches, work 2 double crochets together, repeat from * to end, turn. 12 stitches.

Row 14: Make 1 chain, * work 1 double crochet into next 2 stitches, work 2 double crochets together, repeat from * to end, turn. 9 stitches.

Row 15: Make 1 chain, * work 1 double crochet into next stitch, work 2 double crochets together, repeat from * to end, turn. 6 stitches.

Row 16: Make 1 chain, work 1 double crochet into each stitch.
Fasten off leaving a long length of yarn.

FRONT RIGHT AND BACK LEFT MUD GUARDS (MAKE 2 IN TOTAL)

Using 4mm (US G/6) hook, yarn B and leaving a long length of yarn, make 16 chains.
Row 1: Working into the back loop only, work 1 double crochet into second chain from hook, work 1 double crochet into each chain, turn. 15 stitches.

Row 2: Make 1 chain, work 1 double crochet into each stitch, turn.

Rows 3 – 4: As row 2.

Row 5: Make 1 chain, work 1 double crochet into next 8 stitches, turn. 8 stitches.

Row 6: Make 1 chain, work 2 double crochets together, work 1 double crochet into next 6 stitches, turn. 7 stitches.

Row 7: Make 1 chain, work 1 double crochet into next 5 stitches, work 2 double crochets together, turn. 6 stitches.

Row 8: Make 1 chain, work 2 double crochets together, work 1 double crochet into next 4 stitches, turn. 5 stitches.

Row 9: Make 1 chain, work 1 double crochet into next 3 stitches, work 2 double crochets together, turn. 4 stitches.

Row 10: Make 1 chain, work 2 double crochets together, work 1 double crochet into next 2 stitches, turn. 3 stitches.

Row 11: Make 1 chain, work 1 double crochet into next stitch, work 2 double crochets together, turn. 2 stitches.

Row 12: Make 1 chain, work 2 double crochets together. 1 stitch.
Fasten off.

FRONT LEFT AND BACK RIGHT MUD GUARDS (MAKE 2 IN TOTAL)

Using 4mm (US G/6) hook, yarn B and leaving a long length of yarn, make 16 chains.

Row 1: Working into the back loop only, work 1 double crochet into second chain from hook, work 1 double crochet into each chain, turn. 15 stitches.

Row 2: Make 1 chain, work 1 double crochet into each stitch, turn.

Rows 3 – 4: As row 2.
Fasten off.
With wrong side facing, rejoin yarn B.

Row 5: Make 1 chain, work 1 double crochet into next 8 stitches, turn. 8 stitches.

Row 6: Make 1 chain, work 2 double crochets together, work 1 double crochet into next 6 stitches, turn. 7 stitches.

Row 7: Make 1 chain, work 1 double crochet into next 5 stitches, work 2 double crochets together, turn. 6 stitches.

Row 8: Make 1 chain, work 2 double crochets together, work 1 double crochet into next 4 stitches, turn. 5 stitches.

Row 9: Make 1 chain, work 1 double crochet into next 3 stitches, work 2 double crochets together, turn. 4 stitches.

Row 10: Make 1 chain, work 2 double crochets together, work 1 double crochet into next 2 stitches, turn. 3 stitches.

Row 11: Make 1 chain, work 1 double crochet into next stitch, work 2 double crochets together, turn. 2 stitches.

Row 12: Make 1 chain, work 2 double crochets together. 1 stitch.
Fasten off.

SIDE WINDOWS (MAKE 2)

Using 4mm (US G/6) hook and yarn C, make 8 chains.

Row 1: Working into the back loop only, work 2 double crochets into second chain from hook, work 1 double crochet into next 5 chain, work 2 double crochets into last chain, turn. 9 stitches.

Row 2: Make 1 chain, (work 2 double crochets into next stitch) twice, work 1 double crochet into next 5 stitches, (work 2 double crochets into next stitch) twice, turn. 13 stitches.

Row 3: Make 1 chain, (work 1 double crochet into next stitch, work 2 double crochets into next stitch) twice, work 1 double crochet into next 5 stitches, (work 1 double crochet into next stitch, work 2 double crochets into next stitch) twice, turn. 17 stitches.

Row 4: Make 1 chain, (work 1 double crochet into next 2 stitches, work 2 double crochets into next stitch) twice, work 1 double crochet into next 5 stitches, (work 1 double crochet into next 2 stitches, work 2 double crochets into next stitch) twice, turn. 21 stitches.

Row 5: Make 1 chain, (work 1 double crochet into next 3 stitches, work 2 double crochets into next stitch) twice, work 1 double crochet into next 5 stitches, (work 1 double crochet into next 3 stitches, work 2 double crochets into next stitch) twice, **do not turn.** 25 stitches.

Next Row: Work 1 slip stitch into the end of each row of double crochets, work 1 slip stitch into front loop only of each starting chain, work 1 slip stitch into the end of each row of double crochets. 15 stitches.

Fasten off leaving a long length of yarn.

HEADLIGHTS (MAKE 2)

Using 4mm (US G/6) hook and yarn C make a magic ring.

Round 1: Work 6 double crochets in the magic ring, join with a slip stitch. 6 stitches. Change to yarn D.

Round 2: Make 1 chain, work 2 double crochets into each stitch, join with a slip stitch. 12 stitches.

Fasten off leaving a long length of yarn.

BACK LIGHTS (MAKE 2)

Using 4mm (US G/6) hook and yarn E make a magic ring.

Round 1: Work 6 double crochets in the magic ring, join with a slip stitch. 6 stitches. Fasten off leaving a long length of yarn.

TYRES (MAKE 4)

Using 4mm (US G/6) hook and yarn D make a magic ring.

Round 1: Work 6 double crochets in the magic ring, join with a slip stitch. 6 stitches.

Round 2: Make 1 chain, work 2 double crochets into each stitch, join with a slip stitch. 12 stitches.

Round 3: Make 1 chain, * work 1 double crochet into next stitch, work 2 double crochets into next stitch, repeat from * to end, join with a slip stitch. 18 stitches. Change to yarn F.

Round 4: Make 1 chain, * work 1 double crochet into next 2 stitches, work 2 double crochets into next stitch, repeat from * to end, join with a slip stitch. 24 stitches.

Round 5: Make 1 chain, * work 1 double crochet into next 3 stitches, work 2 double crochets into next stitch, repeat from * to end, join with a slip stitch. 30 stitches.

Round 6: Make 1 chain, work 1 double crochet into each stitch, join with a slip stitch.

Round 7: As round 6.

Round 8: Make 1 chain, * work 1 double crochet into next 3 stitches, work 2 double crochets together, repeat from * to end, join with a slip stitch. 24 stitches.

Round 9: Make 1 chain, * work 1 double crochet into next 2 stitches, work 2 double crochets together, repeat from * to end, join with a slip stitch. 18 stitches.

Round 10: Make 1 chain, * work 1 double crochet into next stitch, work 2 double crochets together, repeat from * to end, join with a slip stitch. 12 stitches.

Begin to stuff tyre.

Round 11: Make 1 chain, * work 2 double crochets together, repeat from * to end, join with a slip stitch. 6 stitches.

Fasten off leaving a long length of yarn.

BUMPER (MAKE 2)

Using 4mm (US G/6) hook and yarn D make 25 chains.

Row 1: Working into the back loop only, work 1 double crochet into second chain from hook, work 1 double crochet into next 23 chain. 24 stitches.

Fasten off leaving a long length of yarn.

SIDE WINDOW DIVIDE (MAKE 2)

Using 4mm (US G/6) hook and yarn A make 2 chains.

Row 1: Working into the back loop only, work 1 double crochet into second chain from hook, turn. 1 stitch.

Row 2: Make 1 chain, work 1 double crochet into next stitch, turn.

Rows 3 – 5: As row 2.

Fasten off leaving a long length of yarn.

MAKING UP

Fill car body with plenty of stuffing and stitch closed. For each mud guard and tyre: close hole on tyres. Attach triangular part of mud guard to car body. Position tyre under mud guard and sew tyre to car body. Sew remainder of mud guard around tyre. Attach side windows, headlights, back lights, bumpers and side window divides. Weave in remaining loose ends.

AEROPLANE

Reach new heights of excitement for your children with this easily constructed aeroplane design. Give your aeroplane a personalized touch by extending the wing length a little, or by altering the colour combinations.

SKILL LEVEL: SOME EXPERIENCE

YOU'LL NEED:

YARN
Deramores Studio DK or any No.3 medium weight yarn
A – 1 x 100g of Mustard
B – 1 x 100g of Burnt Orange
C – 1 x 50g of Light Sky

HOOK
4mm (US G/6) hook

EXTRAS
Toy stuffing

AEROPLANE

SIZE
Length 16cm/6¼in

TENSION
18 sts and 19 rows to 10cm/4in
Measured over double crochet using 4mm (US G/6) hook.

SPECIAL INSTRUCTIONS
When changing to a different colour yarn, work the last two loops of the previous stitch in the new colour.

PLANE BODY
Using 4mm (US G/6) hook and yarn B make a magic ring.

Round 1: Work 6 double crochets into the ring. 6 stitches.

Round 2: Work 2 double crochets into each stitch to end. 12 stitches.

Round 3: * Work 1 double crochet into next stitch, work 2 double crochets into following stitch, repeat from * to end. 18 stitches.

Round 4: * Work 1 double crochet into next 2 stitches, work 2 double crochets into following stitch, repeat from * to end. 24 stitches.

Round 5: * Work 1 double crochet into next 3 stitches, work 2 double crochets into following stitch, repeat from * to end. 30 stitches.

Round 6: * Work 1 double crochet into next 4 stitches, work 2 double crochets into following stitch, repeat from * to end. 36 stitches.

Round 7: Work 1 double crochet into each stitch.

Rounds 8 – 13: As round 7.
Change to yarn A.

Round 14: Working into back loop only, work 1 double crochet into each stitch.

Rounds 15 – 25: As round 7.

Round 26: * Work 1 double crochet into next 4 stitches, work 2 double crochets

together, repeat from * to end. 30 stitches.

Rounds 27 – 28: As round 7.

Round 29: * Work 1 double crochet into next 3 stitches, work 2 double crochets together, repeat from * to end. 24 stitches.

Rounds 30 – 31: As round 7.

Round 32: * Work 1 double crochet into next 2 stitches, work 2 double crochets together, repeat from * to end. 18 stitches. Start to stuff, and continue to stuff as you complete body.

Rounds 33 – 34: As round 7.

Round 35: * Work 1 double crochet into next stitch, work 2 double crochets together, repeat from * to end. 12 stitches.

Rounds 36 – 37: As round 7.

Round 38: * Work 2 double crochets together, repeat from * to end. 6 stitches. Fasten off leaving a long length of yarn and close hole.

WINGS – (MAKE 2)

Using 4mm (US G/6) hook and yarn B make a magic ring.

Round 1: Work 6 double crochets into the ring. 6 stitches.

Round 2: Work 2 double crochets into each stitch to end. 12 stitches.

Round 3: * Work 1 double crochet into next stitch, work 2 double crochets into following stitch, repeat from * to end. 18 stitches.

Round 4: * Work 1 double crochet into next 2 stitches, work 2 double crochets into following stitch, repeat from * to end. 24 stitches.

Round 5: Work 1 double crochet into each stitch.

Rounds 6 – 15: As round 5.

Round 16: Work 1 double crochet into each stitch, join with a slip stitch to start of round. Fasten off leaving a long length of yarn.

PROPELLER

Using 4mm (US G/6) hook and yarn C, make 10 chains.

Row 1: Working into the back loop only, work 2 treble crochets into second chain from hook, work 1 half treble crochet into next 2 stitches, work 1 double crochet into next stitch, work 1 slip stitch into next stitch, work 1 double crochet into next stitch, work 1 half treble crochet into next 2 stitches, work 2 treble crochets into next stitch, **do not turn.** 11 stitches.

Now work in rounds, working into the opposite side of the starting chains, as follows:

Round 1: Working into the back loop only, work 1 treble crochet into next stitch, work 1 half treble crochet into next 2 stitches, work 1 double crochet into next stitch, work 1 slip stitch into next stitch, work 1 double crochet into next stitch, work 1 half treble crochet into next 2 stitches, work 1 treble crochet into next stitch, work 1 slip stitch into next stitch. 9 stitches.

Fasten off leaving a long length of yarn.

TAIL – (MAKE 3)

Using 4mm (US G/6) hook and yarn C make a magic ring.

Round 1: Work 6 double crochets into the ring. 6 stitches.

Round 2: Work 2 double crochets into each stitch to end. 12 stitches.

Round 3: Work 1 double crochet into each stitch to end.

Round 4: As round 3.

Round 5: Work 1 double crochet into each stitch to end, join with a slip stitch to start of round.

Fasten off leaving a long length of yarn.

TYRES – (MAKE 2)

Using 4mm (US G/6) hook and yarn A make a magic ring.

Round 1: Work 6 double crochets into the ring. 6 stitches.

Round 2: Work 2 double crochets into each stitch to end. 12 stitches.

Round 3: * Work 1 double crochet into next stitch, work 2 double crochets into following stitch, repeat from * to end. 18 stitches.

Round 4: Working into the back loop only, work 1 double crochet into each stitch.

Round 5: Work 1 double crochet into each stitch.

Round 6: As round 4.

Round 7: * Work 1 double crochet into next stitch, work 2 double crochets together, repeat from * to end. 12 stitches.
Start to stuff, and continue to stuff as you complete tyre.

Round 8: * Work 2 double crochets together, repeat from * to end, join with a slip stitch to start of round. 6 stitches.
Fasten off leaving a long length of yarn.

MAKING UP

Attach propeller to plane body. Attach tails to plane body. Position wings on plane body and sew in place. Close hole in tyres and attach to plane body. If you feel the wings are not stiff enough, flatten the wings and work some stitches through them, using the hole between the stitches.

TIC-TAC-TOE

The classic board game. Two players take it in turns to place their pieces on the board and the first to get three in a row is the winner! Made out of durable cotton, this game is perfect for all ages.

SKILL LEVEL: EASY

YOU'LL NEED:

YARN

Rowan Handknit Cotton or any No.3
medium weight yarn
A – 2 x 50g of Thunder 335
B – 1 x 50g of Ecru 251
C – 1 x 50g of Celery 309

HOOK

4.5mm (US 7) hook

TIC-TAC-TOE

SIZE

Board measures 27cm/10¾in wide and 27cm/10¾in high

TENSION

12 sts and 9 rows to 10cm/4in
Measured over half treble crochet using 4.5mm (US 7) hook holding yarn double throughout.

BOARD

Using 4.5mm (US 7) hook and yarn A held double make 34 chains.

Row 1: (RS) Work 1 half treble into third stitch from hook, work 1 half treble into each stitch to end. 32 stitches.

Row 2: Make 2 chains, work 1 half treble into each stitch to end.

Rep last row until work measures 27cm/10¾in.
Fasten off.

NOUGHTS – (MAKE 5)

Using 4.5mm (US 7) hook and yarn B held double make 3 chains, join into first chain to form a ring.

Round 1: Make 1 chain, work 6 double crochets into ring, join with a slip stitch. 6 stitches.

Round 2: Make 1 chain, work 2 double crochets into next stitch to end, join with a slip stitch. 12 stitches.

Round 3: Make 1 chain, * work 1 double crochet into next stitch, work 2 double crochets into next stitch, repeat from * to end, join with a slip stitch. 18 stitches.

Round 4: Make 1 chain, * work 1 double crochet into next 2 stitches, work 2 double crochets into next stitch, repeat from * to end, join with a slip stitch. 24 stitches.
Fasten off.

CROSSES – (MAKE 5)

Using 4.5mm (US 7) hook and yarn C held double make 9 chains.

Row 1: Work 1 double crochet into second stitch from hook, work 1 double crochet into next stitch to end. 8 stitches.

Row 2: Make 1 chain, work 1 double crochet into each stitch to end.

Fasten off.

Insert hook into fourth stitch, rejoin yarn and work 1 double crochet into same stitch, work 1 double crochet into next stitch.

Next Row: Make 1 chain, work 1 double crochet into next 2 stitches.

Rep last row once more.

Fasten off.

Work other side to match.

MAKING UP

Press as described on page 17.

GRID – (MAKE 4)

Using 4.5mm hook and yarn B, make 40 chains.

Fasten off.

Using the photo as a guide and a small running stitch, attach the grid to the board.

FISHING GAME

This cute fishing game, worked in a mercerized cotton, will grab any child's attention. Using the rod to catch the fish will keep little ones entertained. A drawstring base keeps it all neat and tidy in one place.

SKILL LEVEL: SOME EXPERIENCE

YOU'LL NEED:

YARN

Rowan Cotton Glace or any No.3
light weight yarn
A – 3 x 50g of Cobalt 850
B – 1 x 50g of Dawn Grey 831
C – 1 x 50g of Persimmon 832
D – 1 x 50g of Mineral 856
E – 1 x 50g of Poppy 741
F – 1 x 50g of Aqua 858

I estimate you will be able to make 3 fish out of 1 ball of yarn.

HOOK

3mm (US C/2) hook

EXTRAS

Small magnets approx. 15mm/½in diameter x 2mm/1⁄16in thick – you will need one for each fish plus an extra one for the rod
Toy magnets
Matching ribbon to the base, 6mm/¼in wide and 130cm/50in long
Bamboo cane approx. 30cm/12in long
Toy stuffing

FISHING GAME

SIZE
Base – 29cm/11½in diameter
Fish – 7cm/2¾in length

TENSION
30 sts and 30 rows to 10cm/4in
Measured over double crochet using 3mm
(US C/2) hook.

FISH
Using 3mm (US C/2) hook make a magic
ring.
Round 1: Work 6 double crochets into
magic ring. 6 stitches.
Round 2: Work 2 double crochets into
each stitch. 12 stitches.
Round 3: Work 1 double crochet into
each stitch.
Round 4: * Work 2 double crochets into
next stitch, repeat from * to end. 24 stitches.
Round 5: Work 1 double crochet into
each stitch.

Round 6: * Work 2 double crochets into
next stitch, work 1 double crochet into next
2 stitches, repeat from * to end. 32 stitches.
Round 7: Work 1 double crochet into
each stitch.
Round 8: * Work 2 double crochets into
next stitch, work 1 double crochet into next
3 stitches, repeat from * to end. 40 stitches.
Round 9 – 14: Work 1 double crochet into
each stitch.
Round 15: * Work 2 double crochets
together, work 1 double crochet into next 3
stitches, repeat from * to end. 32 stitches.
Round 16: * Work 2 double crochets
together, work 1 double crochet into next 2
stitches, repeat from * to end. 24 stitches.
Round 17: * Work 2 double crochets
together, work 1 double crochet into next
stitch, repeat from * to end. 16 stitches.

SHAPE TAIL

Round 18: Work 1 double crochet into each stitch.

Round 19: * Work 2 double crochets into next stitch, work 1 double crochet into next stitch, repeat from * to end. 24 stitches.

Round 20: * Work 2 double crochets into next stitch, work 1 double crochet into next 2 stitches, repeat from * to end. 32 stitches.

Round 21: * Work 2 double crochets into next stitch, work 1 double crochet into next 3 stitches, repeat from * to end. 40 stitches.

Round 22: * Work 2 double crochets into next stitch, work 1 double crochet into next 4 stitches, repeat from * to end. 48 stitches.

Round 23: Work 1 double crochet into each stitch.

BASE

Using 3mm (US C/2) hook and yarn A make a magic ring, work 6 double crochets into ring.

Round 1: Make 1 chain, work 2 double crochets into each stitch. 12 stitches.

Round 2: Make 1 chain, * work 1 double crochet into next stitch, work 2 double crochets into following stitch, repeat from * to end, join with a slip stitch. 18 stitches.

Round 3: Make 1 chain, * work 1 double crochet into next 2 stitches, work 2 double crochets into next stitch, repeat from * to end, join with a slip stitch. 24 stitches.

Round 4: Make 1 chain, * work 1 double crochet into next 3 stitches, work 2 double crochets into next stitch, repeat from * to end, join with a slip stitch. 30 stitches.

Round 5: Make 1 chain, * work 1 double crochet into next 4 stitches, work 2 double crochets into next stitch, repeat from * to end, join with a slip stitch. 36 stitches.

Round 6: Make 1 chain, * work 1 double crochet into next 5 stitches, work 2 double crochets into next stitch, repeat from * to end, join with a slip stitch. 42 stitches.

Round 7: Make 1 chain, * work 1 double crochet into next 6 stitches, work 2 double crochets into next stitch, repeat from * to end, join with a slip stitch. 48 stitches.

Round 8: Make 1 chain, * work 1 double crochet into next 7 stitches, work 2 double crochets into next stitch, repeat from * to end, join with a slip stitch. 54 stitches. Continue to work as above, working 1 double crochet more on each round before increase, until you have 43 rounds/264 stitches, join with a slip stitch to start of round. Fasten off.

MAKING UP

Drop your magnet into the nose of the fish, then stuff the body well with toy stuffing. I didn't stuff the tails.

Holding the tail together, join the end by weaving a tapestry needle through the tops of the stitches.

Thread the ribbon onto a tapestry needle and using a running stitch go around the edges of the base, spacing 5cm/2in between inserting your needle.

ROD

Using 3mm (US C/2) hook and yarn B make 40 chains.

Row 1: Work 1 double crochet into fourth chain from hook, turn, make 4 chains, work 1 double crochet into second chain from hook, work 1 double crochet into next 5 stitches. 6 stitches.

Next Row: Make 1 chain, work 1 double crochet into next 6 stitches.

Repeat last row 3 times more.

Next Row: Slip stitch into the next 3 stitches, make 1 chain, work 1 double crochet into next 36 stitches made from initial chain.

Fasten off leaving a tail approx. 30cm/12in long.

MAKING UP

Sew a running stitch around edge of crocheted piece, place magnet against fabric and pull tight to close.

Wrap tail around one end of bamboo cane and secure by threading the end under the wrapped stitches.

TOY BASKET

This basket can either be used for storing your baby changing essentials or for toys in the nursery. Worked holding two strands together to create a dense fabric and using gender neutral colours, this basket will look good in almost any room.

SKILL LEVEL: SOME EXPERIENCE

YOU'LL NEED:

YARN
Rowan Handknit Cotton or any No.4 medium weight yarn
A – 3 x 50g of Slate 347
B – 3 x 50g of Ecru 251

HOOK
6mm (US J/10) hook

TOY BASKET

SIZE

72cm/28¼in circumference and 22cm/8¾in high

TENSION

12 sts and 10 rows to 10cm/4in
Measured over half treble crochet using 6mm (US J/10) hook and yarn held double throughout.

BASKET

Using 2 strands of yarn A held together and 6mm (US J/10) hook make 4 chains, join with a slip stitch into first chain made to form a ring.

Round 1: Make 2 chains (this counts as 1 half treble crochet), work 9 half treble crochets into ring. 10 stitches.

Round 2: Make 2 chains (this counts as 1 half treble crochet), work 2 half treble crochets into each stitch, join with a slip stitch into second chain. 20 stitches.

Round 3: Make 2 chains (this counts as 1 half treble crochet), * work 2 half treble crochets into the next stitch, work 1 half double crochet into the next stitch, repeat from * to end. Join with a slip stitch into second chain. 30 stitches.

Round 4: Make 2 chains (this counts as 1 half treble crochet), * work 2 half treble crochets into the next stitch, work 1 half double crochet into the next 2 stitches, repeat from * to end. Join with a slip stitch into second chain. 40 stitches.

Round 5: Make 2 chains (this counts as 1 half treble crochet), * work 2 half treble crochets into the next stitch, work 1 half double crochet into the next 3 stitches, repeat from * to end. Join with a slip stitch into second chain. 50 stitches.

Round 6: Make 2 chains (this counts as 1 half treble crochet), * work 2 half treble crochets into the next stitch, work 1 half double crochet into the next 4 stitches, repeat from

* to end. Join with a slip stitch into second chain. 60 stitches.

Round 7: Make 2 chains (this counts as 1 half treble crochet), * work 2 half treble crochets into the next stitch, work 1 half double crochet into the next 5 stitches, repeat from * to end. Join with a slip stitch into second chain. 70 stitches.

Round 8: Make 2 chains (this counts as 1 half treble crochet), * work 2 half treble crochets into the next stitch, work 1 half double crochet into the next 6 stitches, repeat from * to end. Join with a slip stitch into second chain. 80 stitches.

Round 9: Make 2 chains (this counts as 1 half treble crochet), * work 2 half treble crochets into the next stitch, work 1 half double crochet into the next 7 stitches, repeat from * to end. Join with a slip stitch into second chain. 90 stitches.

Round 10: Make 2 chains (this counts as 1 half treble crochet), work 1 half treble into each stitch through front loop only. Join with a slip stitch into second chain.

Rounds 11 – 13: Make 2 chains (this counts as 1 half treble), work 1 half treble into each stitch to end. Join with a slip stitch into second chain.

Break off 1 strand of yarn A and join in 1 strand of yarn B.

Rounds 14 – 17: Make 2 chains (this counts as 1 half treble), work 1 half treble into each stitch to end. Join with a slip stitch into second chain.

Break off remaining strand of yarn A and join in second strand of yarn B.

Rounds 18 – 29: Make 2 chains (this counts as 1 half treble), work 1 half treble into each stitch to end. Join with a slip stitch into second chain.
Fasten off.

MAKING UP
Sew in loose ends.

HOUSE DOORSTOP

This doorstop is a fun décor item for your child's bedroom. Worked in a DK light weight yarn, you can bring colours from your bedroom theme or create a contrasting house design. You could always make a few of these doorstops, in different colour designs, to create your very own little row of terraced houses.

SKILL LEVEL: SOME EXPERIENCE

YOU'LL NEED:

YARN
Rowan Baby Merino Silk DK or any No.3
light weight yarn
A – 2 × 50g of Straw 671
B – 1 × 50g of Iceberg 699
C – 1 × 50g of Candy 695
D – 1 × 50g of Leaf 692

HOOK
3mm (US 2/3) hook

EXTRAS
Toy stuffing

HOUSE DOORSTOP

SIZE
26cm/10¼in high × 14cm/5½in wide

TENSION
25 sts and 29 rows to 10cm/4in
Measured over double crochet using 3mm (US 2/3) hook.

BASE AND SIDES
Using 3mm (US 2/3) hook and yarn B, make 36 chains.

Row 1: Work 1 double crochet into second stitch from hook, work 1 double crochet into each stitch to end. 35 stitches.

Row 2: Make 1 chain, work 1 double crochet into each stitch to end.
Repeat last row until base measures 12cm/4¾in, ending with a wrong side row.

**Join in yarn A.
Next Row: Make 1 chain, work 1 double crochet into each stitch to end.
Repeat last row 5 times more.
Change to yarn B.
Next Row: Make 1 chain, work 1 double crochet into each stitch to end.
Repeat last row 5 times more.
Change to yarn A.
Next Row: Make 1 chain, work 1 double crochet into each stitch to end.
Repeat last row 5 times more.
Repeat last 12 rows twice more.
Fasten off.

With right side facing, work opposite side to match from **.

FRONT AND BACK PANELS

***Using 3mm (US 2/3) hook with right side facing and yarn A, work a row of 35 double crochets along side edge.

Next Row: Make 1 chain, work 1 double crochet into each stitch to end.
Repeat last row until work measures 14.5cm/5¾in, ending with a wrong side row.
Next Row (RS): Make 1 chain, work 2 double crochets together, work 1 double crochet in each stitch until 2 stitches remain, work 2 double crochets together. 33 stitches.
Next Row: Make 1 chain, work 1 double crochet into each stitch to end.
Repeat last 2 rows until 1 stitch remains.

With right side facing, work opposite side to match from ***.

ROOF

Using 3mm (US 2/3) hook and yarn C, make 36 chains.
Row 1 (RS): Work 1 double crochet into second chain from hook, work 1 double crochet into each stitch to end. 35 stitches.
Row 2: Make 1 chain, work 1 double crochet into each stitch to end.
Repeat last 2 rows until roof measures 28cm/11in, ending with a wrong side row.
Fasten off.

MAKING UP

Press as described on page 17.

DOOR

Using 3mm (US 2/3) hook and yarn C, make 15 chains.
Row 1 (RS): Work 1 double crochet into second chain from hook, work 1 double crochet into each stitch to end. 14 stitches.

Row 2: Make 1 chain, work 1 double crochet into each stitch to end.
Repeat last 2 rows until door measures 10cm/4in.
Fasten off.

BUNTING FLAGS – (MAKE 3)

Using 3mm (US 2/3) hook and yarn D, make 2 chains.
Row 1 (RS): Work 1 double crochet into second chain from hook. 1 stitch.
Row 2: Make 1 chain, work 2 double crochets into next stitch. 2 stitches.
Row 3: Make 1 chain, work 2 double crochets into next 2 stitches. 4 stitches.
Row 4: Make 1 chain, work 2 double crochets into next stitch, work 1 double crochet into next 2 stitches, work 2 double crochets into next stitch. 6 stitches.
Row 5: Make 1 chain, work 1 double crochet into each stitch to end.
Fasten off.

Using 3mm (US 2/3) hook and yarn D, make 3 chains, * with right side facing slip stitch across 6 stitches of top of flag, make 2 chains, repeat from * twice more, make 1 chain.
Fasten off.
Using photo as a guide and matching yarn, attach the door and bunting to front of house. Join all 4 sides of house using mattress stitch. Attach roof to house, stuffing firmly as you go.

INDEX

A
Aeroplane 130

B
Bean Bags 74
Bunny Rabbit 42

C
Car 122
Cloud Cot Toy 28
Colour Game 88
Comfort Blanket 20
Crochet Basics 7
    Decreasing 12
    Double crochet 7
    Half treble crochet 8
    Increasing 11
    Joining in a new colour 10
    Joining two pieces together – crochet 14
    Joining two pieces together – mattress stitch 13
    Making a magic ring 15
    Slip stitch 10
    Treble crochet 9
    Working stitches into a magic ring 15
Crochet terminology 16
    Crochet hook sizes and conversions 16
    UK / US terminology conversions 16

E
Elephant 58

F
Finger Puppets 102
Finishing Instructions 17
Fishing Game 138

G
Giraffe 52

H
House Doorstop 146

L
Loop Rattle 18

N
Number Disks 94

O
Octopus 48

P
Pressing 17

S
Sensory Toy 70
Skittles 117
Stacking Cubes 84
Stacking Rings 78
Star Mobile 33
Stitching 17
Super Soft Ball 112

T
Teddy Bear 36
Tension 17
Tic-Tac-Toe 134
Toy Basket 143

U
Unicorn 64

ACKNOWLEDGEMENTS

I would like to thank everybody who has helped me bring this book together. My designers who made it possible and created projects for use within the book:

Lucy Pollock – Teddy Bear, Bunny Rabbit, Octopus, Giraffe, Elephant and Unicorn
Chanelle Hudson – Stacking Rings
Ana Yogie – Car and Aeroplane
Nichola Corbin – Skittles
Alexa Templeton – Finger Puppets

Special thanks also go to the team at Rowan for endorsing my book with yarn sponsorship. Finally, I would like to thank the team at GMC and Quail for bringing my ideas to life and making this book possible.

Emma Osmond

To order a book, or to request
a catalogue, contact:

GMC Publications Ltd
Castle Place, 166 High Street,
Lewes, East Sussex,
BN7 1XU
United Kingdom
Tel: +44 (0)1273 488005
www.gmcbooks.com